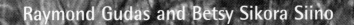

Raymond Gudas and Betsy Sikora Siino

Doberman Pinschers

Everything About Purchase, Care, Nutrition, Training, and Behavior

With Full-color Photographs
Illustrations by Michele Earle-Bridges

D1019458

BARRON'S

CONTENTS

DOBERMANS AT LARGE

Say the words **Doberman Pinscher**, *and the image of the mad, snarling guardian of the junkyard immediately pops into mind. Or the mad, snarling dog next to a sneering Nazi in World War II. Or the mad, snarling attack animals patrolling the billionaire's estate. See a pattern here?*

Every time we think of a Doberman, we see the sleek, gleaming coat, the hard, muscular physique, the ears alert to the most inaudible hint of intrusion, the dark, intelligent eyes, and of course, the snarl, the mad aggression, and the teeth.

Indeed, the Doberman is one of the world's most recognizable breeds and, because of the nature of that recognition, one of the most feared. This leaves one to wonder just how much of that reputation is deserved, and how much has been manufactured through years of stereotyping in film and on television. The Doberman has been a willing actor, but one that has been fatally typecast as the guard dog, the Nazi collaborator, the unstable protector of the realm. Even a top-flight Hollywood agent would be hard-pressed to change this breed's image to that of sitcom family pet.

Its rich history and commanding presence make the Doberman Pinscher a dynamic companion for those owners who are properly prepared for the task.

But somewhere in the middle of these two images—vicious guard and loving companion—we find the true Doberman Pinscher, the dog that has inspired generations of dog lovers to choose this beautiful, noble animal as both pet and family protector. To the right owner, the right family, the Doberman offers the best of all worlds, but as we will see, not everyone is up to the job.

History of the Doberman

As the owner or potential owner of a Doberman Pinscher, it is important that you have at least a general awareness of the history of this noble breed. This will help you better understand what a remarkable animal this dog is, and the proud tradition it represents.

Early Developments

The Doberman's story begins in the early 1880s in the German province of Thuringia—specifically, the area around the town of

Apolda—where a certain Herr Karl Louis Dobermann made his home.

A man of many responsibilities, Herr Dobermann served as the local tax and rent collector, a policeman and occasional night watchman, and, as fate would have it, a caretaker of the area's dog pound. In the course of his involvement with the many animals under his supervision, he gradually became obsessed with developing a special new breed of guard dog to protect him while he performed his various duties.

Although Herr Dobermann was not in the habit of maintaining records of his work, it is widely accepted that the so-called German

The Doberman was the result of a breeding program in its German homeland, carried out for the creation of a fearless dog that would excel in all areas of protection, including military and police work.

Pinscher, an aggressive guard-type dog common in Germany at the time, provided the basis for his experiments. Other breeds also played a role in the Doberman Pinscher's evolution, most notably the Rottweiler, as well as, among others, the German Shorthaired Pointer, the Weimaraner, the Manchester Terrier, and the Great Dane.

The result of Herr Dobermann's efforts was an alert, muscular, medium-size dog, initially black in color, and fearless in disposition. The animals came to be known locally simply as "Dobermann's dogs," but they were also called "Thuringian Pinschers," Thuringian referring to the dog's home province, pinscher being the German word for "terrier." From this mix came the name "Doberman Pinscher," the second "n" in Dobermann dropped in many parts of the world. Except in the United States, the term "pinscher" was later dropped, as well, because it was decided the name "terrier" was inappropriate for this breed.

Rise in Popularity

A new dog breed doesn't come along every day, of course, and the arrival of the Doberman caused considerable excitement. During the early 1900s, Dobermans began appearing throughout Europe, as far east as Russia, and as far west as the United States. The Doberman's future looked very bright indeed—until the onset of World War I, which would devastate the breed's numbers in Europe. Many

Doberman breeders who could not bear the thought of seeing their animals' lives wasted in war, sold their stock to dog fanciers in other parts of the world, especially to those in the United States. This spurred the breed's climb to international prominence.

The breed in Germany began to recover somewhat after the war, but foreign sales continued. World War II would virtually bring an end to exportation, but by that time the breed was on firm footing in many countries. Today, the Doberman Pinscher is found on every continent, as are the many specialty clubs that continue to advance the breed. None, however, is more active than the Doberman Pinscher Club of America, founded in 1921.

Military and Police Service

The Doberman's alert and fearless nature, coupled with his strength, agility, loyalty, and quick learning ability, made him ideal for military and police work. Though a relative newcomer to this kind of work, the breed's performance has been spectacular.

By the start of World War I, the Germans had recruited several thousand dogs, including Dobermans and German Shepherd Dogs, trained for guard and rescue duty. The British, too, had successfully instructed dogs to work in similar capacities. Real strides in the art of canine warfare came during World War II. During the war, dogs—the Doberman prominent among them—were recruited by both sides, the U.S. Armed Forces commissioning at least 250,000 canine warriors, and the Marines Corps later adopting the Doberman as its official mascot. War dogs were trained for tracking, scouting, sentry and patrol duty, locating wounded, supply caches, and snipers in the

---

TIP

A Word of Warning

Contrary to some opinions, it is usually not a good idea to train a Doberman pet for attack or protection work, especially a Doberman in a household with children. Nor should one choose this breed to feed some sort of macho image, which, sadly does occur far too often. In keeping with this, one must never try to foster aggression in this dog in the misguided "hope" of making it a better guard.

---

field, detecting mines and other booby traps, physically attacking the enemy, and guarding prisoners.

Given its origins, the Doberman was as likely a candidate for police work as it was for military duty. Today, the use of dogs in military and law enforcement capacities overlap in many areas: patrol work, crowd control, sniffing out narcotics or explosives, tracking, and the subjugation of human adversaries.

Dogs for such work are initially selected on the basis of age (five years usually being the limit), height, weight, health, condition, and learning ability. Candidates must also exhibit a certain level of aggression in their behavior, not to the point of uncontrollable viciousness, but a certain amount of brazen bravado. Dogs that are lethargic and take no interest in strangers, or that are easily approached and coaxed into tail wagging and friendship— indeed, the kind that most of us might like to have as a pet—must be summarily dismissed as

The more realistic you are about the Doberman's potentially aggressive nature, the better equipped you will be to determine whether this is the right breed for you and your family.

potential canine police cadets. Like the human officers with whom they are partnered, police and military dogs must be incorruptible.

Training for the Private Sector

In the private sector, Dobermans have been worked in just about every capacity imaginable—advanced obedience training, for exam-ple, as well as therapy work in nursing homes and hospitals—though their use as guard dogs continues to head the list.

Potential Doberman owners are wise to choose this breed for its companion qualities first, protection qualities second. Most qualified trainers and behaviorists warn against attack or protection training a family pet, and indeed, with the Doberman, protection is all part of the package. Invite the dog in as a full-fledged family member, which really is all this very social, sensitive dog wants anyway. Treat your pet with respect and guide it with proper, consistent training, and the animal's mere presence in the home is enough to keep criminals at bay.

The Role of Instinct

Only an extraordinarily multitalented dog can accomplish so many tasks with such aplomb, and the individual Doberman Pinscher may meet these goals only in the care of someone who understands the breed and what is required to appropriately harness its talents and energy. This begins with acknowledging the Doberman's own special brand of canine instinct and channeling it in a positive direction. Once you choose this breed, dedicate yourself to the noble end goal of understanding its particular world view as both a breed and an individual, and you will both enjoy a closer bond.

Exactly how much of a dog's behavior is inherited and how much is learned is a debate that remains unsettled, except to say that both sides of the equation seem very much involved. One expects a Doberman Pinscher to be fearless and loyal, a "natural" watchdog, the same way one would expect a bird dog to take to water or a Greyhound to running. Of course, not all dogs turn out the way we expect. Certainly those dogs that have been mentally or physically abused or improperly trained or

Intelligent, enthusiastic, and loyal, Doberman Pinschers have been trained effectively for such vocations as pet therapy and service work.

TIP

Hot Spots

Pets can develop "hot spots" (skin inflammations caused by a dog biting himself incessantly) or lick granulomas (chronic skin infections caused by habitual licking), as the result of inconsistent relationships with their owners or a stressful lifestyle. A stressed pet may also be prone to problems with their auditory, respiratory, gastrointestinal, reproductive, and urinary systems, and an animal that isn't feeling well may be likely to lash out at those who love him. Whenever a dog behaves abnormally then, both medical and emotional causes need to be explored.

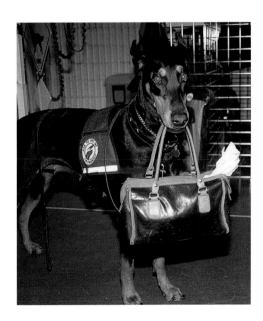

Dobermans are as breathtaking to look at as they are devoted to their duties.

contribute to the dog's long-term health—all very good reasons to make the effort. If you don't have the time or the inclination for this, then perhaps the Doberman, or any dog, is not right for you.

Dominating Other Animals

Many dogs, harking back to the pack-oriented social structures of their ancestors, have a tendency to dominate other animals (and, if given the opportunity, people), instinctively competing for status and position. To be sure, certain breeds, the Doberman among them, exhibit this tendency more than others. While some breeds seem not to show even a hint of such behavior, all engage in some form of ranking and/or assessment of their "peers."

The inclination starts early. Even while puppies are still confined with their littermates, they will routinely engage in play-fighting with their siblings, exploring their own physical capabilities and those of their friendly and usually willing adversaries. It's all a game at this stage, but in a real-life pack situation, the day would come soon enough when more assertive members of the group would begin to confront each other, vying for position in the pecking order of their extended family.

When two adult dogs square off in a contest of dominance, the competition isn't over until one of the two runs away, or in a more ritualistic display of submission, the weaker animal rolls over onto his back or side and willingly exposes his throat to the victor. The action communicates surrender; in fact, it's all that is usually needed to stop the advances of the winner.

handled can exhibit behavioral extremes that exceed the bounds of normalcy (not all that unusual, unfortunately, for Doberman Pinschers that are too often purchased for all the wrong reasons). Our personal input as dog owners, therefore, is crucial—*especially* with a potentially aggressive and powerful breed like the Doberman.

Taking an interest in your Doberman's behavior will go a long way in helping you establish and maintain a sound and happy relationship with your pet. Not only will it enhance your appreciation and enjoyment of your pet and his breed, it will also facilitate training and

The Stress Factor

Needless to say, no one really wants to run into a stressed Doberman, and indeed stress is a primary source of health problems in pets. While some may believe the typical family dog leads a charmed and carefree life, stressful situations can arise at any time.

As has been presumed with the human reaction to stress as well, if a dog reacts confidently to external threats to his well-being, he may also be less susceptible to germ threats internally. Conversely, if a dog reacts to some perceived threat with extreme fear, his internal defense mechanisms—antibodies, white blood cells, and other components of his immune system—may be slow to respond when they are most needed. This temporary lapse in the body's defenses may be all that is needed for the onset of some illness that may otherwise have been avoided.

Because people and other animals are a major part of a pet's environment, negative changes in those relationships can cause all kinds of behavior and health problems. Excessive fear, emotional frustration, continuous confinement, inconsistent training, or the introduction of a new pet, are almost all guaranteed to manifest themselves in some demonstrative, probably destructive, way.

Mating rituals and pregnancy can also be a great source of stress. Dogs are more likely to fight during mating season, hormonal changes can make dogs nervous and irritable, and a pregnant female is bound to be more irritable,

Despite its dramatic history, all any Doberman wants is a valued position in a loving family and people who respect what a special breed it is.

increasing the potential for abnormal behavior. Physically, a dog may eat and sleep less and burn up more energy when his reproductive juices are flowing, thus placing a greater burden on the animal's internal defenses. Conversely, some dogs may suffer a lack of appetite and actually appear to be ill.

Many canine behavior problems can also be traced to changes in a pet's owner's behavior. As sensitive as they are, dogs pick up on our moods and attitude changes, and sometimes they can even be adversely affected by them, either because they are afraid of the behaviors and treatment, or they fear that such negative feelings are signaling a change in their status within the family. Your Doberman must be shown through your actions and your consistent behavior toward him that he is an accepted member of the family, with his own rightful share of food, territory, attention, love, and confidence-building training.

An alert owner can recognize when his or her dog is happy, sad, afraid, angry, confused, curious, frustrated, hopeful, and even affectionate, by picking up on obvious, and not-so-obvious, clues. When you learn to interpret your Doberman's behavior, you will better understand that this complex animal is communicating a wide variety of attitudes and desires.

Body Language

Declaring dominance: Body posture, facial expressions, eye contact, and tail movement are important clues to a Doberman's, and any dog's, state of mind. For example, an aggressive dog vying for dominance stares intently at other animals around him. His head and ears are held high, the hair along his spine may bristle, and his tail (even the Doberman's docked tail) will be held rigid in a straight line with his back. The dog's entire body appears stiff and tense. The animal will look at his opponent with a fixed stare, at the same time circling the opponent with a slow, cautious movement that is very different from the kind displayed during a casual encounter. Remember, too, that dogs tend to consider a human stranger's stare in the eyes to be a provocative, aggressive signal, which can have dire consequences, hence the reason so many children are bitten in the face by strange dogs.

Acknowledging submission: A submissive dog will react by turning his eyes and head downward or away from his tormentor's stare to acknowledge inferiority and submission, and to avoid an escalation of conflict. Only two dogs of equally high levels of confidence and perceived position will maintain their stares until an actual fight erupts to determine ultimate superiority.

Readiness to attack: When a dog is about to attack, his mouth opens slightly and his muzzle wrinkles to expose his teeth. Snarls and growls accompany the reaction, although some dogs attack silently—or from a distance, in which case, they tend to freeze momentarily, with the head held low and level with the back, the tail wagging slowly from side to side. Some dogs sink into a prone position before making their initial assault.

Dog fights: Fights vary in intensity, but they usually consist of more bravado than bloodshed. The most serious battles are likely to be those between dogs of the same sex. A female out of breeding season may, however, feel compelled to drive off an unfamiliar male, snapping and

Acknowledging submission.

growling at him with as much ferocity as she can muster, even though it is rare that any serious harm is intended. It is abnormal, however, for a male dog to attack a female.

Puppies are generally safe from the attack of adults. It's as if their elders understand that youngsters can't really be held responsible for their sometimes boisterous behavior. Some dogs, however, are less tolerant than others, and they will bite a bothersome pup.

The Language of Sounds

Barking, growling, whining, moaning, and other sounds make up what is a rather complex canine language system. Many dogs have little need to make sounds because their other communication signals are correctly interpreted by us, but the better one understands his or her Doberman pet, the quieter the home environment is likely to be.

Some dogs can be quite vocal. This is especially true of fearful dogs or even of confident Dobermans that never seemed to learn that as guards they need to be selective about what deserves a barking tirade, and what doesn't. If you carefully study the different sounds your pet makes at different times, you may eventually begin to have a pretty good idea of what your Doberman is trying to tell you.

Preparing to attack.

Deeper, louder sounds typically indicate aggression and dominance, while softer, higher-pitched sounds represent submissiveness and perhaps fear. This can apply to humans as well. People who speak to dogs in an overly soft and sentimental voice are in effect assuming a submissive position before the animal. This can send confusing signals to a dog that is supposed to be under your control—especially a dog such as the Doberman, which must be under your control. As much as your dog may adore you, he may also decide that given your submissive behavior, perhaps he needs to become the dominant, or alpha, member in the relationship.

We have explored the history of the Doberman Pinscher, and where the breed fits both within the family of dogs and within society as a whole. Now it's time to get to know the Doberman on a more intimate level so you can determine how, and if, he can fit into the day-to-day life of your family.

The Doberman as a Pet

When most people chance upon a Doberman—whether the dog is walking obediently at his owner's side or simply resting within the confines of his yard—the overriding reaction is the sounding of a silent mental alarm, a reminder that, should he mark you as a foe, here is an animal capable of inflicting serious bodily injury. No doubt it is the common perception of the Doberman's role as a police, guard, and junkyard dog, as well as his portrayal on television and in film, that heighten this perception—a perception that is not entirely unfounded. A strong and fearless animal bred originally as a guard, the Doberman is more than capable of defending himself, his master, and anyone his master designates.

While the Doberman is obviously not the ideal choice for every dog owner, his fierce reputation is only half this breed's story. In qualified and capable hands, the Doberman

Life is never boring when one chooses to live with a Doberman Pinscher.

can also make for a lovable and truly outstanding companion. In fact, the Doberman is first and foremost a family dog, which thrives best when invited to reside indoors with his family so he might participate in all the family's activities. Thrown out into the yard day in and day out to guard the premises will only lead to a sad, lonely, and neurotic Doberman Pinscher. But helping the Doberman achieve his goal as ultimate family dog requires proper preparation and commitment on the part of the owner, and a sound understanding of the dog's basic nature and character.

Behavioral Characteristics

While every dog, like every dog owner, must be evaluated as an individual, the Doberman, like all pure breeds, possesses clear behavioral characteristics that are common to the truest representatives of the breed.

Despite some arguments to the contrary, the Doberman rates about average in the category of emotional stability when compared to other

Keeping this very athletic, energetic dog busy can help prevent annoying, potentially dangerous problems that can arise when a dog is inactive and unchallenged.

breeds. While he does not generally display the relative cool of, say, the Newfoundland or the Labrador Retriever, neither is he known to be as high-strung as such breeds as the American Cocker Spaniel or the Irish Setter.

The typical Doberman's most exceptional characteristics are those that have molded his watchdog and guard dog abilities. Properly nurtured, these traits can make the Doberman a valued member of the household.

✔ A Doberman will bark when confronted by an intruder, sounding the alarm to his family as any good watchdog will do. But many a Doberman will also display a willingness to take matters into his own paws (or teeth) should he perceive a threat, and he may do so with an eagerness that is generally unrivaled among his working-dog counterparts. This is a testimony not only to the Doberman's self-confidence and alert mind, but also to the dog's legendary tenacity.

✔ The Doberman also tends to be very territorial, as anyone who has ever been on the receiving end of his guardian instincts can testify. He eagerly defends what he perceives to be his own or his family's territory.

✔ Not unrelated is the fierce loyalty the breed displays to his family members, despite the fact that some Dobermans may tolerate the abuses of children better than others, or that some

The American Kennel Club recognizes Dobermans with both cropped and natural ears. The practice of ear cropping, however, is illegal in many countries.

Owners must diffuse a Doberman Pinscher's natural sense of territoriality and loyalty so that these behaviors, and any potentially dangerous behavioral characteristics, don't spin out of control.

may exhibit a noticeable degree of preference for a particular member of the family.

Neither behavior must be allowed to spin out of control, or you end up with a stereotypical example of the breed. But this need not occur. The Doberman rates very high in learning ability, which means he can and should be trained to behave properly. When handled with respect, confidence, and consistency, this dog is a fast and willing learner.

Forceful and vigorous by nature, the Doberman may display a certain intensity in any number of activities, whether reacting to adversity or simply running around during play. Some breeds—for example, the Bloodhound and the Greyhound—are active hounds outside, but become relatively inactive indoors. And occasionally, as with such dogs as the Shih Tzu, the Pug, and the Bichon Frise, the opposite occurs. The Doberman, on the other hand, holds a steadier course, conducting himself with high energy outdoors and maintaining a moderately high activity level inside the home, as well.

Are You Right for the Doberman?

Given our exploration of the Doberman Pinscher, fairness demands that some considerations be given to the basic nature of the person who wishes to live with a Doberman pet, as well. Simply put, a dominant and energetic dog, which the Doberman certainly is, needs an equally dominant and energetic owner. Otherwise, both dog and owner are likely to live to regret the matchup.

A dominant dog: Proper nutrition, health care, grooming, exercise, and companionship are critical components for the well-being of any dog, but some dogs can present more of a challenge than others to even the most devoted owner. While some dogs are naturally submissive in nature, others do all they can to try and take over their household and family. A very dominant dog, particularly a dog bred specifically to guard and protect his family, may become difficult when he wants his way, and in some instances may even display viciousness when getting his "demands" across. It takes an owner with a certain resolve, confidence, and know-how to keep such a bold and capable animal in line. One of the most important steps

CHECKLIST

Ear Cropping

1 Cropping involves surgical trimming and suturing of the ear's edge, usually done when a puppy reaches about seven weeks of age.

2 The procedure requires general anesthesia and must be done only by a licensed veterinarian (it is illegal for a breeder, groomer, or any layperson to do the procedure), preferably one highly skilled, who can create the proper shape and length of the ideal Doberman ear.

3 The ear must then be carefully posted, taped, cleansed, and medicated every day to make sure it is properly "trained" to stand erect and is protected from infection. The fledgling owner is wise to purchase a puppy from a breeder who will see him through the weeks, sometimes months, of cropping follow-up care.

a newcomer to the Doberman breed can take is to commit from day one to his or her pet's formal training and socialization, preferably done with a professional trainer who knows, understands, and likes the Doberman breed.

Exercise: A large, active, energetic Doberman needs regular exercise, and thus an owner who is willing and able to offer that to the dog. It would be unkind and unhealthy to deny a dog such as the Doberman the physical activity he so naturally craves. Simply throwing the dog out in a fenced backyard to exercise himself won't suffice.

Commiting to the breed: And finally, remember that when you take a Doberman as a pet, you commit not only to that particular dog, but also to his entire breed. Given the Doberman's often well-deserved negative reputation, it will be your job to act as a strong ambassador for the breed, to convince those you and your pet meet that there is much to be admired and respected in this dog. Help the dog convince the public that in the right hands, he is a solid, loyal canine citizen. You must take a vow of responsible ownership, and make sure that you, your family, and your dog live up to that vow.

Ears and Tails

The Doberman's character should be first and foremost on your mind when deciding whether you and this breed are right for each other, as should his need for exercise, activity, firm training, and the dog's natural desire to be an integral member of the family. But there are also some physical characteristics unique to this dog that should be given some consideration: namely, cropped ears and docked tails. While tail docking is accepted by most owners, you need to decide between a natural-eared Doberman or one that is altered in the name of tradition.

Those high peaked ears often considered the signature of the Doberman Pinscher, the ears fanciers claim give the dog "the look of eagles," do not occur naturally. That look, dominant, though not required, among Dobermans in the American show ring, is the product of a long and sometimes arduous medical procedure that requires careful attention from the veterinarian, the breeder, and the new owner. Not so the docked tail. When a Doberman puppy is

Successful ear cropping, a process that can take months to complete, requires a commitment to proper "training" of the ear, as well as diligent hygiene to prevent infection.

about three days old, his tail is "docked," that is, cut and sutured at the second joint or so, as dictated by the breed's standard. On such a young puppy, there is minimal pain, and healing is quick. The ears, however, require more attention, and a lot more time.

The practices of cropping ears and docking tails have been around for centuries, particularly among working breeds. A docked tail and cropped ears were allegedly less likely to get in the way of a dog's work. In the case of the Doberman, the lack of long ears or tail gave a perpetrator less to grab onto in the heat of an attack. From the very beginning Dobermans sported this look, and today, purists seek to keep the tradition alive.

While tail docking does not usually top the list of controversial animal-welfare subjects, ear cropping has its share of critics. In fact, the practice is outlawed in many parts of the world, including most of Europe, but it remains the norm among Doberman Pinschers in the United States. Though the Doberman's American breed standard allows for a natural ear in the show ring, the majority of show Dobermans sport a cropped ear.

There are those who would like to see cropping made illegal in the United States just as it is in other countries, but to date, American Doberman fanciers have a choice. While some cannot imagine a Doberman without cropped ears, others find the natural ear infinitely charming. Both camps are free to remain true to their preferences, but they should learn all they can ahead of time before making the decision.

Dogs and Children

Plenty of children have grown into adulthood safely beside beautiful, well-trained Doberman Pinschers, and they can imagine no other canine companion. You must, however, make sure that your children, and any children who visit your home, are trained properly in interacting with dogs in general, and with this breed in particular.

This process must begin long before the Doberman, even an adorable, seemingly harmless 10-week-old puppy, ever sets foot in the household. Like any animal, this dog is a creature that must be respected by everyone in the

Though natural ears are acceptable in the American show ring, cropped ears are by far the dominant style.

participating in his training classes, and taking the dog for walks (once you are sure the youngsters can control the animal). The kids should also learn not to sneak treats to the dog from the table, or to offer cookies and hot dogs when Mom and Dad aren't looking. Participation of this kind is sure to foster a friendship between child and dog that can last a lifetime.

Adjusting to Other Pets

When deciding on a Doberman, you must also think about the other pets in your home. Plenty of households host multiple dogs, and even a variety of pet species, but you cannot underestimate or ignore the challenges of ensuring that the kingdom remains peaceful.

Given time, and a little judicious input on your part, a Doberman puppy will usually adjust to other dogs in a family household with a minimum of trauma. There are exceptions, however, and chief among these is the introduction of a second female into a home already occupied by an older female. Adult female Dobermans tend to become possessive of their masters as they grow older, and they may resent the new arrival to the point where they will display aggression. With some effort on your part, the two should eventually learn to accept—or at least tolerate—each other. If not, you may have to change the arrangement; you can't spend your life as a referee for two animals that want to tear each other apart.

✔ To reap success as peacemaker, you should introduce a newcomer to an existing canine

family, and everyone must learn to treat the dog consistently, firmly, and kindly.

The kids must learn that it is wrong to bother the animal while he is eating or sleeping, or to pull his ears or tail or otherwise mistreat him, even in play. If your puppy comes to you with newly cropped and taped ears, the kids must learn that they are not to bother those ears or encourage the puppy to play too roughly. Teach them, too, that if the puppy stops playing, they must respect that and stop, too, allowing the puppy time to rest and take naps, privately and quietly. Otherwise, the Doberman may respond by biting, possibly causing serious injury in extreme cases, and he may develop a negative impression of children that could carry on into adulthood. Keep those early experiences positive.

The sensible approach is to let children participate in caring for the dog: changing his water, brushing him (under your supervision),

Starting at a very early age, a Doberman puppy must learn to channel its energies appropriately to prevent problems later on.

pet on neutral ground, perhaps a beach or park where neither dog has been before.

✔ Keep the two separated when no one is at home, at least for the first few months, but allow them to come into frequent contact with one another when you are there to supervise them.

✔ It is equally important to avoid any hint of favoritism toward either animal, which means supplying them with separate feeding dishes, toys, and beds.

✔ Feed both Dobermans the same food at the same time (comparably smaller amounts for the older dog so she doesn't exceed her normal daily intake of calories), perhaps in different rooms.

✔ Walk the two together when this is possible, since puppies will not be able to "go the distance" with an adult dog.

✔ Play with them together, though not in a way that the animals end up competing for the same toy. Jealousies can arise when one of the animals, usually the older dog, sees the other as a rival, or worse, as her replacement.

Cats and Dobermans

While a large dog such as a Doberman should never come in contact with pocket pets such as hamsters or mice, which have been known to die of fear in those instances, helping a dog and cat to adjust to each other generally presents problems only if both are fully grown. In this case, there may be an uneasy period of adjustment, but the two should learn to live together in time. If they don't, they will need to be separated at all times for the protection of the resident cat.

On the other hand, introducing a young puppy to a resident adult cat should present little trouble, and puppies and kittens typically make friends easily in the course of play.

With proper socialization and respect, the Doberman can become an integral part of any family activity.

CHOOSING WISELY

Deciding that the Doberman Pinscher is your destiny is only the beginning. The first real step toward making this relationship a success is to choose the right Doberman, and that can take some work.

A Challenging Quest

Your first course of action should be learning as much as possible about the Doberman breed from books and the Internet. When it's time to see some Dobermans in the flesh, attend dog shows where you can see a variety of the dogs together in one place (contact local kennel clubs, groomers, veterinarians, and the American Kennel Club for information on these events).

The more time you spend studying Dobermans, at shows or elsewhere, the better you'll appreciate true quality when you see it on the street—or, more important, when it's time to select a dog for yourself. Talk to handlers, breeders, veterinarians, Doberman Pinscher Club representatives, breed rescue people, and responsible Doberman owners, who can answer your questions and broaden your knowledge of this breed. Mentioning that you are interested

Choosing a puppy carefully is the first step toward a successful owner-Doberman relationship.

in acquiring a Doberman is often all you'll need to get the conversation started, as many of the people you're likely to meet at shows are breeders, aspire to be breeders, work for breeders, or can recommend breeders.

Don't forget, though, that everyone has preferences and prejudices. That is why you should resist any temptation to buy a puppy from the first breeder you talk to. No matter how dedicated and knowledgeable he or she may appear to be, no matter how healthy or handsome the puppies for sale may seem, inspect at least a few other litters and talk to other breeders before making a final decision about a dog you hope will be a part of your life for many years to come.

Since Dobermans are available in several coat colors (black, red, blue, and fawn; whites are marketed, but not recognized officially by the breed and the AKC), it's a good idea to see and get to know them all. The more you look around, the better your chances of finding the best dog for you and your family.

Both show-quality and pet-quality Doberman Pinschers can make fine pets. Top-notch breeders specialize in both.

Your Honorable Intentions

Now we come to an important question: What is the best Doberman for you? If, like most people, you're simply looking for a good family dog—a healthy animal and a true representative of the breed—you can find what you're looking for from a variety of sources: a breeder, a breed rescue organization, or sometimes even at an animal shelter.

Of course, some Dobermans are more expensive than others. A puppy from top-of-the-line champion stock, for instance, will command more than a pet-quality pup, but remember that this latter animal from a responsible, ethical breeder will benefit from the same care and health considerations that resulted in his show-quality brethren. And there is ample middle ground between the two. For instance, if you have serious plans to enter the show ring and engage in a limited amount of breeding, or if you simply want to obtain a better-than-average dog, you can spend more than the going rate and hope to get a better dog for your money (though there are no guarantees).

Breeding: If you are committed to the prospect of becoming a full-time breeder, dreaming, perhaps, of some day producing a dynasty of champions, you would be well advised to acquire a Doberman of genuine aristocratic status, whatever the cost. The breeder of such an animal, however, may insist that you first prove yourself worthy of the animal by working with another dog and learning the ropes, with the breeder as mentor. Likewise, if you spend a small fortune for a show-quality Doberman but have absolutely no intention of entering him in competition, what is the point? Serious fanciers, in fact, would consider it a sin to deny a potential champion his chance at greatness.

Price: Though you are likely to get what you pay for when selecting a Doberman, that is not always the case. Indeed it is senseless to look for "bargains" when purchasing a Doberman, or to make a selection based on price alone. Pricing in the dog-selling business can be quite competitive, especially where popular breeds such as the Doberman are concerned.

While there is every chance you will wind up paying a great deal for a puppy of lesser quality from a pet store (not a preferred or even safe source of sound Doberman puppies), you might also be offered a "bargain puppy" from a store that is trying to unload an older, not-so-cute-anymore puppy. There is also a good chance that this dog is a product of a "puppy mill," a breeding operation that churns out unhealthy puppies taken from their overbred mothers at too young an age. You might soon discover that your bargain Doberman is riddled with health problems and a bad temperament. Is it worth the risk?

Rescue groups or animal shelters: Depending on what you are looking for, another source to be seriously considered is the breed rescue group or even the animal shelter. Every day, perfectly lovely purebred Dobermans are surrendered to dedicated people who make it their mission to find loving and permanent homes for these animals. Should you choose to work with one of these, find one where the rescuers get to know the unique characteristics of each animal in their charge (do they like children? cats? loud noises? men?), preferably by living with them in foster situations. The rescuer should, in turn, be just as diligent in learning all he or she can about the would-be adopter (those seeking junkyard dogs need not apply), to ensure that the right dog ends up with the right owner.

Where to Begin Your Search

Whatever your specific intentions, begin by looking in your local phone book, which may list Doberman breeders and kennel clubs in your area. You'll also find listings in various dog magazines and on the Internet, but remember that what is stated in an ad or online may not quite describe the truth about a kennel and the quality of its dogs. Don't overlook the classified

ad sections of the newspapers serving your community either. While you will find listings here from so-called amateur "backyard breeders," whose motivation might be a fast buck rather than genetics and temperament, so can you find ads from bona fide experts in your area, as well. You can also contact the national breed club for assistance and referrals. The corresponding secretaries of such organizations, now easily accessible online, can supply would-be puppy buyers with breeder referrals in their home areas.

Do not hesitate to look further if you decide the pickings in your area are slim, or if you are intrigued by the reputation of more prominent breeders elsewhere. Today, transporting animals by air is both safe and reasonably priced. Top breeders are accustomed to this practice, and

If your goal is to take your Doberman to its championship in the show ring, you will need to work with a reputable show breeder who is equally willing to work with you.

most are more than willing to assist their buyers in this endeavor to ensure that a puppy arrives at its destination safely and soundly.

Naturally, it's always best to see and examine the Doberman puppy you are buying for yourself, as well as the home or facility where he was whelped and raised. If, however, you can't or don't want to fly or drive to the source, but are "sold" on the animal's bloodline and on the integrity of the breeder—and on his or her written guarantee of satisfaction (a must)—you can complete the transaction long distance. Note, however, that the success of such a venture, or any puppy-buying or dog-buying experience, hinges on your clearly and honestly communicating about the type of Doberman you want, as well as your long-term goals, if any.

Once you find a breeder who you believe is a good match, you may have to wait a while for the type of puppy you want. Most reputable

A puppy should not be taken from his mother until he is at least eight weeks old. Any younger, and the pup may not be able to bond effectively to a human family.

breeders maintain waiting lists for their pups, and they are usually impressed by puppy buyers who have a clear idea of what they want—for instance, a pet-quality pup with natural ears—and are willing to wait for it.

Of course, even the best-laid plans and the noblest of intentions do not always bring the anticipated results. Not even the breeder, who knows his or her stock better than anyone else, can promise you that a particular Doberman is destined for any specific measure of greatness. Only time will tell, and much depends on nutrition, training, and the general care the animal receives after he has arrived at his new home. You can improve the odds of success by educat-

Spaying

If you have ever heard the notion that a female must have at least one litter to achieve emotional fulfillment or similar nonsense, forget it! Such assertions are simply wrong, and they do nothing but lead to the production of more unwanted puppies that will never find loving, permanent homes. If anything, spaying is a kindness to the female pet and to the canine population at large.

Neutering the Male

The same can be said about neutering the male dog. The altered male is a better, more attentive pet, because he is more interested in the well-being and activities of his family than in scouting the neighborhood for females or obsessively marking his territory. Males, also, enjoy long-term health benefits from neutering, as the procedure helps to prevent various illnesses and cancers in the years to come.

ing yourself, choosing both Doberman and breeder wisely, and avoiding impulse or pity buys.

Buyer Beware

Though there are always risks in choosing a new pet, there are certain precautions you can and should take that will at least help to reduce the risks of your ending up with a problem pet.

Removing the Puppy from His Mother

First of all, don't even consider taking a puppy home that has not yet been weaned, a process that typically occurs at about six weeks of age. To separate one so young from his mother is cruel and indefensible, and if the puppy has not yet been fully introduced to solid foods, the animal's health and survival are placed in needless jeopardy. A breeder that would part with a puppy so young is also one to avoid.

It is widely believed that removing a puppy from the litter too soon can affect the animal's psychological development. It is therefore best to wait until the animal is older—eight weeks or more—before removing him from the security of his initial surroundings. In fact, an ethical breeder won't even let a puppy go until he is at least eight weeks old, which not only covers the weaning issue and the ear cropping issue, the surgery for the latter occurring when the puppy is seven to nine weeks of age, but also launches the stage in the puppy's development when he is most open to bonding with a human family.

Male or Female?

The sex of a Doberman can account for behavioral differences between dogs. Males, for example, may tend to be more assertive than females. As such, they can sometimes be more difficult to house-train, are more inclined to fight with other dogs, and are more likely to roam if the opportunity presents itself. While there are always exceptions, females, on the other hand, may be more gentle and affectionate, and thus a better candidate for a family pet. Not that there is anything wrong with a first-time Doberman owner or a family with children choosing a male puppy; the dog may simply require more diligent training and discipline.

Neutering

In either case, male or female, surgical alteration can help make the chosen Doberman a

Those who do not care to deal with the challenge of raising a puppy may be able to find an older pet from a show breeder or a responsible rescue organization.

better pet, and alleviate some of the problems that can arise when a dog is more concerned with mating rituals and thus other dogs than he is with his human family. For example, if you choose a female and are certain you will never want to show or breed the animal, it's best that you have her spayed. This will do more than relieve you of the burden of unexpected pregnancy; it will likewise eliminate the twice-yearly periods of sexual "heat" when furniture and carpet staining are a concern. At the same time it will curtail the annoying antics of lovesick males that might lay siege to the perimeter of your home. It is also well documented that spaying virtually eliminates the female's risk of developing mammary, or breast, cancer, along with other forms of female-oriented cancers, as she grows older, the best reason of all to have this simple and inexpensive procedure performed.

What About an Older Dog?

Not everyone wants the responsibility of raising a puppy, and you may either seek or unexpectedly run across a fully grown Doberman available for sale or adoption. Older Dobermans are available from rescue groups or from breeders who wish to place retired show dogs ready for a life of leisure. Should you consider this? Well, that depends.

If you have had no previous experience with dogs—powerful, potentially domineering dogs, especially—and you do not intend to put your heart and soul 24/7 into learning and practicing what is required to make the relationship a success, then the answer is a definite no. However, if you are willing, and you believe an older Doberman is the dog for you, you might want to opt for the retired show dog, which, we hope, is already trained and properly socialized. The rescue Doberman, on the other hand, can present a variety of challenges depending on his past experiences. Unless you really know what you are doing, and the rescuer with whom you are dealing really knows the dog in question, you may be asking for trouble. Retraining a fully grown Doberman that may be scarred by his past, and gaining his confidence and respect, is often a long and arduous, and sometimes even dangerous, process. It requires a level of knowledge and understanding that few novices possess.

The advantage of buying a Doberman puppy is that you start with a clean slate. You have a direct hand in early training and initiating the animal into your family's life. There is much to be said for the bonds of love and loyalty that such an arrangement fosters, but indeed the Doberman is a candidate for that love and loyalty, regardless of his age. Whether you are seeking a puppy or adult Doberman, the key is working with a breeder or rescuer you trust, someone whose overriding goal is to see the animal land in a loving permanent home.

Choosing a New Best Friend

You have done your homework, you have found a breeder you trust, and you are meeting a litter for the first time. This is no time to let down your guard. Buying a puppy, a companion to spend the next decade or more beside you, is serious business. Impulse has no place here. What to look for:

General behavior: In terms of general behavior patterns, normal, well-adjusted Doberman puppies should be alert, active, and instinctively curious about what goes on around them. Indeed, your arrival should stimulate consider-able activity in the puppies you are visiting to evaluate as potential companions.

Maternal behavior: Be vigilant as you evaluate the little family you have come to meet. First, observe the quality of the mom's maternal behaviors toward her pups, as she is the one that first teaches the young ones how to be dogs, and wields great influence. As for the puppies, you will recognize right away which of the siblings are more dominant and which are more submissive, which tend to initiate play, and which tend to cower at the invitation. Which would you label shy and which would you consider aggressive? These traits will

A wise choice involves evaluating a puppy's behavior, appearance, and relationship with his mother and siblings.

While you may find puppies irresistible, try to choose your new pet with your head rather than your heart.

become only more prominent as the pup matures if the new owner does not know how to intervene effectively.

Personality type: While extreme shyness and viciousness are undesirable in any pet, they are ultimately a matter of degree. Your choice of personality types may range from a seemingly easygoing Doberman that is more disposed toward obedience, to the dog that tends to be more spirited and thus presents an exciting challenge to the more experienced owner. It is most important that the Doberman fit in with your own personality and lifestyle.

Shyness: If one or more pups in the litter are cautious about approaching you, it could just mean they don't know what to make of you yet. This is especially likely with younger puppies that have had little contact with people. Some friendly and reassuring posturing from you should help to bring them around. If, over time, however, a particular puppy continues to cower and shiver in the corner, suppress the sympathy and look elsewhere.

Health: Take the time to evaluate health, as well. Does the puppy appear to be of properly proportioned weight? An extremely thin

physique can be a sign of ill health, a poor appetite, and nutritional deficiency. Obesity— another sign of poor nutrition—can be the sign of health problems, or be the result of an inferior diet consisting of poor ingredients and inappropriate treats.

Diet and coat: Diet also plays a part in the look of the animal's coat, which in a healthy puppy should be shiny and clean, the thicker the better. A dull coat can mean a vitamin deficiency. A dirty coat deserves comment too. In the worst case this may suggest a lack of attention from the puppy's caretakers that could extend to other areas of the puppy's care as well. Inspect the animal's skin by parting the hair with your fingers or slowly rubbing your hand against the coat's grain. You should not find parasites, sore, dry scales, or any frequency of insect bites. Check the anal area, too, for signs of diarrhea or inflammation.

Eyes and teeth: The puppy's eyes should be clear and free of discharge, the lids and rims dark. The dog's gums should be pink and even in color, the teeth bright and clean. Brown stains on teeth indicate that the dog may have had distemper, in which case the stains are permanent. Also inspect the alignment of the teeth. You are looking for a true scissor bite, with the lower incisors touching the inside of the upper incisors.

Genetic problems: Ask the breeder about the dog's diet, his vaccine and worming status, and any health problems he may have had. Ask, too, about genetic certifications for eye problems and hip dysplasia, both of which ethical breeders test for. In fact, ask about any genetic problems that may exist in the puppies' family, such as wobbler syndrome, a severe neurological condition common in Dobermans, and von Willebrand's disease, a bleeding disorder also common in the breed.

Heart condition: Ask as well about dilated cardiomyopathy, a fatal heart condition that is presumed to be hereditary and is all too common in Dobermans. Affected dogs must not be used for breeding, and it is the wise buyer who asks ahead of time.

Ear cropping: Now is also the time to discuss ear cropping. If the puppy's ears are to be cropped or have already been done, ask about the follow-up care required to prevent infection and pain and to ensure the best results.

If you want a Doberman with cropped ears, make sure the breeder is confident and knowledgeable about this sensitive subject (a backyard breeder is not likely to be), and work only with a breeder who has the procedure done *before* the puppy moves on to join his new family. Be warned, too, that while a puppy should probably remain with the breeder for the first two weeks or so after the surgery, some breeders won't even part with a puppy until he is three or four months old, to ensure that the ears have been properly trained and have healed under the breeders' own guidance. However, if you would rather your puppy's ears remain natural, discuss that with the breeder as well. He or she should respect your decision.

If the pup's ears have been cropped, make sure you leave with specific instructions on the care

If you prefer a Doberman with natural ears, work with a breeder who respects your choice.

of those ears. As we have discussed, cropped ears require a great deal of care and attention on the part of owners to foster a clean, sharp line and a lack of infection. Assuming he or she lets the puppy go before the ears are healed, the reputable breeder works closely with his or her

TIP

When to Bring the Puppy Home

Plan to bring your new dog home early in the day if possible. This will give him time before nightfall to explore his new home. The animal may even get tired enough to sleep through the night without yelping or howling, which puppies recently separated from their littermates are likely to do—but don't count on it.

puppy buyers to help ensure that those ears heal as correctly and as painlessly as possible.

Pedigree: And while you're at it, ask to see the dog's pedigree—and the sire and dam, too, if they are on the premises. The ethical breeder will not be offended by any such questions or requests; he or she should instead be impressed that you have done your homework and are taking this choice of companion very seriously.

Evaluating the Breeder

While you are evaluating the puppies, you should also evaluate the puppies' breeder. Ask about his or her experience, goals, and breeding philosophy. Make sure the emphasis of the program is on temperament as well as appearance, and steer clear of a breeder who hedges on the subject of genetic conditions that affect the breed.

✔ The serious, reputable breeder will riddle you with questions about how you intend to care for the dog and the type of home and lifestyle you will provide.

✔ He or she should be very concerned about why you have chosen this breed. Do you intend to train him carefully and consistently?

✔ Will the dog reside with the family, or do you intend to keep him tied out "protecting" your property?

AKC Registration

The subject of American Kennel Club registration should also arise. First, the reputable breeder knows that AKC recognition does not equal quality or health, only that a puppy's parents were both registered members of a given breed. Second, the breeder will certainly want to know if you are seeking a pet puppy or a show prospect. If you are a newcomer to showing, the breeder may be willing to mentor you in taking a show puppy to his championship, and full AKC registration will be a necessity.

The breeder may, on the other hand, choose to offer what is called "limited registration" to puppies going to pet homes. Breeders now have this option to ensure that their nonbreeding-quality puppies will receive AKC recognition, but if they produce puppies, their offspring will not be eligible for registration. Pet-quality puppies are best spayed, neutered, and sent to loving pet homes.

Closing the Deal

Breeders and rescuers with permanent placement in mind should allow you to have the puppy or dog you select examined by a veterinarian of your choosing before the sale is officially completed. The veterinarian will be able to evaluate the animal's general health and his potential for normal development.

The seller of a dog that is eligible for AKC registration is required to provide you with the

Evaluate a breeder's home as well as the breeder. Healthy, well-balanced dogs come from clean, calm, well-organized environments.

necessary application form, or at the very least, a written and signed statement including all the information you will need for that purpose: the breed, sex, and color of the Doberman being registered, the dog's date of birth, the name of the breeder, and the registered names and numbers of the sire and dam. This information will permit you to proceed on your own in the absence of official applications. If the litter you have inspected has already been registered with the AKC, the assigned litter number is what you'll need. If the seller cannot meet these requirements at the time of the sale, you should not proceed with the transaction.

Health Contract

The reputable breeder will also seal the deal with a contract outlining genetic health screening results for eyes, hips, wobbler syndrome, and von Willebrand's disease; spaying and neutering requirements (if any); registration information (limited versus full); return clauses; dietary guidelines; and any other pertinent information. The contract, or lack thereof, reveals the breeder's ultimate motivations in engaging in the messy and very expensive practice of breeding dogs.

Taking Your Pet Home

If you are transporting your pet to his new home by car, avoid unnecessary stops that prolong what may be a frightening or uncomfortable experience for the animal. This is no time to run errands, to shop for puppy supplies (you should already have done that), or to drive all around town to show your friends your new pet. The trip may be less stressful for the puppy if you transport him in a crate, equipped with soft bedding and perhaps a safe chew toy. The puppy may already have had experience with crate training with his breeder, and the crate can offer a sense of security on the journey to his new home.

Bring someone with you so that one of you can keep an eye on your Doberman while the other watches the road. If you are facing a long trip, stop occasionally to offer food and/or water to the animal and for bathroom breaks. Finally, depending on the weather, make sure your car's heater or air conditioner is in proper working order.

BRINGING UP DOBIE

As silly as it might sound, many people first buy a dog, and only then realize that the animal will need a place to sleep, bowls for food and water, a collar and leash, and all the other trappings inherent in responsible dog ownership. All too often, this means a hasty and incomplete last-minute shopping spree.

Needless to say, waiting until the last minute to buy essentials for your new puppy results in chaos and stress during the first few days of the dog-owner relationship, chaos and stress that can easily be avoided by planning ahead.

Sleeping Quarters

The Bed and Bedding

You should probably start with a bed, preferably a bed that will be kept indoors. Many misguided folks believe that large dogs should be outdoor-only dogs. What these individuals do not understand is that virtually every dog wants and needs to be a part of his family, which means spending some time indoors and some time out. While you might provide your Doberman with a comfortable doghouse, so

Doberman Pinschers are enthusiastic, high-energy dogs who require owners with similar characteristics.

should you provide your pet with an indoor sleeping area, as well. You'll sleep better, too, with this arrangement. Indeed, who wouldn't sleep better with a Doberman snoozing in the house?

A well-stocked pet supply store will have at least several types of beds to choose from, ranging from the simplest floor mats, to fluffy cedar-filled pillows, to fanciful basket-type configurations. Whichever style you choose for your pet, consider one that is large enough to accommodate a full-grown Doberman. On the other hand, you might want to begin with something more expendable, preferably washable, during the initial house-training stage. That's fine, so long as the bed is kept dry, clean, and comfortable. Although animals instinctively avoid eliminating in their own sleeping quarters, puppies aren't exactly known for neatness—or great bladder control—so you might want to start with shredded newspapers and a soft old towel as your puppy's first bedding. Replacement is easy and inexpensive, the

towel can be thrown into the washer, and you can always switch to better materials when the animal has matured.

The Dog Crate

Another option is the dog crate. Often a puppy or dog will come from his breeder into his new home already crate-trained, and already viewing its crate as a safe, comfortable sanctuary, providing a cozy, warm, comfortable nook for napping, playing quietly, or even escaping for a while from the attentions of the family. The crate can also provide the owner with an easy option for confining the dog when the family is not at home. Those who sing the crate's praises further laud its role as a valuable tool in housetraining, and a safe compartment in which the dog can travel by car and plane. The crate must not, however, be abused. It should be kept clean

Do your new puppy a favor: Gather her supplies and discuss her care routine with your family before you bring her home.

and well padded, and the dog should not be kept crated for long periods of time.

Placement

Ideally, the crate or bed should be positioned out of the way of major foot traffic, but where it can offer some view of adjoining rooms, so the dog doesn't always have to get up to investigate every sound. Dogs seem to appreciate being able to survey their surroundings without having to abandon the warm embrace of a comfortable sleeping area.

In addition, the bed should be placed in an area of the house that can be confined, such as a laundry room that can be blocked off with a baby gate, or a corner of the kitchen that can be enclosed by an exercise pen. For his own safety and to prevent household damage, a puppy should not be offered free run of the house when no one is home to supervise his activities. Confining his sleeping area will prevent this and foster the puppy's sense of security. For obvious reasons, you should also avoid placing the bed near a radiator or other heat source, or in an area subject to drafts.

It is important for your Doberman to know that he has at least one place in the house that is truly his own. His sleeping area represents such a place—his own piece of turf, a kind of safety zone where he is secure and beyond interference. Take the time to determine the ideal location for the bed at the outset, rather than changing your mind later on and moving it somewhere else, which will only annoy and confuse your pet.

The Feeding Regimen

Your new pet will be facing numerous changes when he first joins your household. It would be wise and kind if diet is not one of them. Before taking the animal home, find out what he is being fed, as well as his current feeding schedule. Duplicate these as closely as possible, at least initially. You can gradually switch to an alternate feeding plan after your Doberman has begun to adjust to his new surroundings.

Collars and Leashes

The Collar

Your puppy will need a collar—several before he is fully grown—and a leash to go with it. You can choose from a wide variety of collars,

---

TIP

Food and Water Bowls

Food and water bowls should be large enough to accommodate a Doberman when he is fully grown.

✔ Made of steel, ceramic, or plastic, the bowls should be of sufficient weight and of such design that they will not be overturned or moved around when they are being used.

✔ Find a convenient out-of-the-way place for the bowls, and try to keep it as a permanent site.

✔ Clean the bowls regularly, and make sure that a fresh supply of water is always within the animal's reach.

---

as long as your choice fits properly. The "rule of thumb" is that you should be able to fit a finger through the collar rather easily as it rests on the dog's neck, but not much more than that.

You can find collars in all sorts of styles, made of leather, nylon mesh, cotton fabric, etc. It is safest to purchase a regular buckle collar for the dog for everyday wear.

Training collars: Reserve training collars for just that—training. Training collars include the metal prong collar, which, unfortunately is seen on far too many Dobermans as an everyday collar (and is probably too severe a tool for most of the Dobermans you see wearing them for training), and the metal choke chain.

The choke chain: The choke chain must be positioned properly on the dog's neck so that

The chain training collar must be placed correctly on the dog's neck to prevent injury and to ensure effective training communication.

when the leash is held loosely, the collar hangs loose, as well. In the course of training, the dog learns that when the leash is snapped, thus tightening the chain around the neck, the dog must obey the command from the person on the other end of the leash. When he obeys, the collar loosens again. Use this collar only for training, however, to prevent the collar from catching on something and injuring the dog when he is unsupervised.

Harnesses: Also available, particularly for walking, are H-shaped harnesses, which can offer stability to both dog and walker, and head halters, which control the dog much as a halter controls a horse, but they must be used correctly to avoid discomfort and injury. When a collar shows the strains of wear, replace it with a new one; replace a collar the dog outgrows as well.

I.D.

The I.D. tag: Don't neglect one of the prime uses of the collar—a place for the dog's identification tag. Should you somehow get separated from your Doberman, a tag on its collar will significantly improve your chances of getting him back. Purchase the tag as soon as you take possession of your new puppy, and from then on, make sure your pet always wears a tag, complete with current information.

Tattoos: It is also becoming increasingly common for owners to have their dogs tattooed for identification purposes, typically around the groin area or on the inside of the

---

TIP

Using a Leash

✔ Purchase the leash early on and introduce it right away.

✔ Snap it onto your puppy's collar and allow the youngster to drag it around a bit to adjust to the feel of a tool that will some day provide him time in the great outdoors with the people he adores most.

✔ Praise the dog for tolerating the strange item; praise him even more when he walks along with you on the other end. In time, the dog will learn that the leash is his ticket to greater freedom.

ear (preferably the former as the latter is too easily, and violently, removed by thieves). The procedure is painless and inexpensive, and the number is registered with agencies that can match lost or stolen dogs to the information maintained by the registry. Tattoos are accepted in the show ring, and they have provided very good results.

Microchipping: Also gaining popularity these days is the microchipping of dogs, in which a microchip containing owner information is implanted under the dog's skin. Should the lost dog be found, a scanner can read the information required to get the dog back to his owner. Animal control officials routinely check recovered dogs for tattoos and microchips, so if your pet should fall into their hands and is so identified, they'll find you.

If you do opt for the tattoo and/or the microchip, don't forgo the tag on the collar, however. The tag is the first place people look, and it's simply that much more insurance that you won't lose your best friend.

The Leash

The main consideration in choosing a leash for your pet is its length. It should be long enough to allow the dog ample exercise on his daily walks, but not so long that you lose control of the dog. Many people you encounter while walking your pet may not appreciate your big, beautiful Doberman running ahead of you to greet them along the way. A shorter leash, one about 6 feet (1.8 m) in length, should meet your needs, and still permit you

Both puppies and adult dogs should wear properly sized collars, complete with current identification tags, at all times.

to maintain the good public reputation of which the Doberman is so in need.

Leashes are typically made of leather, nylon, cotton, and metal chain, but metal is not the best choice. A puppy is likely to chew on his leash, and a metal chain can damage his teeth. For an older Doberman, a floppy, noisy metal chain leash will not provide the structure often required for communication between dog and walker via the dog's leash.

Grooming Supplies

Though the Doberman's short coat might be relatively easy to care for, the dog still requires regular care to keep the coat gleaming and the skin healthy. To keep your pet's coat looking its best, you should brush it regularly (see more on

═══ TIP ═══

Safe Toys

Buy playthings that are sturdy, well made, and labeled as being made especially for dogs to ensure that your pet will not be exposed to toxic materials. Also, keep in mind that plastics can splinter, latex can tear off and block a dog's airway, and metal parts can harm teeth or be swallowed.

grooming in the next chapter). A brush with hard bristles works best. You might also purchase a curry-comb-type tool such as the kind used for horses to stimulate the skin and to foster the coat's shine. Round out your grooming supply list with a flea comb, nail clippers, and a styptic pencil (in case you cut the nails too vigorously). Eventually you will need to purchase flea-control products, as well, but

Provide your puppy with a collection of safe toys to accommodate teething irritation as well as natural puppy energies.

it's best to wait until the puppy is older and you have consulted with your veterinarian.

Toys

Typical dog toys—beef or nylon bones, rope toys, rawhide chews, rubber balls, stuffed fleece dolls, and so on—do more than simply entertain a dog. In addition to providing a remedy for boredom and stress, they also facilitate exercise, and in the case of safe chew toys, contribute to healthy teeth and gums as well.

Teach your new pet, too, what he is allowed to regard as his toys. A young puppy will view anything in his path as free game for his insatiable chewing impulses during his teething stage, and an older dog may do the same when he feels compelled to chew during times of stress. Make sure that you keep valuables, the kids' toys, shoes, and anything else you would like to preserve out of the puppy's reach. If you do catch the pup attacking something forbidden, replace the item with one of the puppy's own toys, and praise the animal for turning his attention to it.

Indoor/Outdoor Dog

Being a member of the family is all any dog wants, and the ideal living arrangement for the canine family member is one that involves time spent both indoors and outdoors.

The Dog Run

Commit to daily walks and exercise with your pet—rain, shine, or snow—but remember, too, that sometimes a dog just likes to loll around in the yard on its own in peace and quiet, listening to the birds and guarding the yard from neighborhood cats. This is not to say you must have a fully contained yard in order to qualify for Doberman ownership, and of course, just throwing the dog out into the backyard every day will not satisfy the dog's exercise requirements. If you don't happen to have a fully fenced yard, you can provide your pet with a dog run (the bigger the better), which can be outfitted with a secure door or gate, toys, clean water, and a doghouse or similar shelter that will protect the dog from direct sun and inclement weather. Here the dog may be safely left to his own devices for an hour or two until it's time to leap back into the family activities. Most Dobermans adapt quite well to such a lifestyle (make sure, though, to bring the dog in when he is ill, or when the weather is too hot, or the temperature drops below freezing).

The Doghouse

No single pet supply store can be expected to carry more than a few doghouse models, so shop around. Make sure the house's design features allow for proper ventilation in hot weather and the retaining of body heat during winter months, as well as keeping snow, rain, direct sun, and wind at bay. The shelter must also be large enough; your Doberman should be able to stand upright or lie fully outstretched inside it. Other commendable features include a durable surface, adequate insulation, a roof that is slightly extended for extra shade, slanted for improved air circulation, and hinged or removable for easy interior cleaning, a slightly raised lip at the foot of the doorway to keep bedding in place, and perhaps even an extended front "deck" so your pet can lie at least partially outside.

═══ CHECKLIST ═══

Playtime Tips

1 Resist the urge to give your dog old shoes, socks, towels, or household articles to play with. Doing so may send the wrong message to the dog, and you may come home some day to find that your pet has been foraging for new playthings around the house.

2 Resist, too, the urge to play tug-of-war with your dog. Many behaviorists believe this simply fosters dominant behavior in a dog, even in a young puppy.

3 Teaching a Doberman Pinscher to prove and exercise his dominance over his family members is probably not the wisest move.

The shelter must, of course, be kept clean and dry, so clean it periodically with hot water and a mild disinfectant, and change the bedding whenever necessary. For bedding you might use cedar shavings, which are available at any pet supply store and are soft and highly absorbent, or clean straw, either of which can be topped with a clean blanket for extra familiarity.

Ideally, the shelter should be placed in a spot that is neither completely exposed to the constant rays of the sun, nor swallowed in permanent shade. It is also recommended that you raise the structure up off the ground slightly to guard against moisture damage.

If you decide to build a doghouse yourself, incorporate these same design elements, and

Most Dobermans are naturally protective of home and hearth, but you must regard them as valued family members as well as family protectors and care for them accordingly.

use hardwoods and nontoxic (lead-free) paint. You can even obtain a blueprint design from animal rescue organizations or the local library.

The Yard

As for the yard itself, carefully inspect the perimeter to ensure that the yard is escape-proof, whether by jumping, digging, or climbing. As an additional precaution, it would be wise to place a "Beware of Dog" sign on every gate to give everyone fair warning of the animal's presence. You may even consider buying locks for the gates, both to prevent accidental incursions into your yard and, however unlikely in a Doberman's case, to provide an extra safeguard against "dognapping." Locks also eliminate the possibility of someone leaving the gate unlatched.

Beware of Doberman

Which brings us to another option that someone without a fenced yard or a dog run may be inclined to consider: tying the dog out in the yard. An easy option, you say. Inexpensive. Convenient. But heed this warning: *Don't do it!*

Tying Up the Dog

We have all had the experience of walking by a house with a dog tied outside to a stake in the ground. In most cases, it is not a pleasant moment. Even if afforded ample length of rope, chain, or leash, a dog so confined can go stir crazy after a while, testing the limits of the leash that holds him to the stake, barking incessantly, growing increasingly irritated as people, dogs, paperboys, and mail carriers pass the house. This can be destructive to even a well-trained Doberman, which, feeling frustrated by this "teasing" mode of confinement, might not appreciate the innocent child who approaches simply because he or she wants to "pet the nice doggie." In this case, neither dog nor child is protected, and the results can be devastating.

Invisible Fences

The same can be said for Dobermans held on their property by so-called invisible fences, those electronic systems that zap a dog by way of a mechanism on the dog's collar, should the

animal venture beyond what he is trained to understand as his boundary. Such a system may or may not keep the dog in the yard—the dog may decide that risking the zap is worth the freedom—and it certainly won't keep other dogs or trespassers out. A dog such as the Doberman (and many would say *any* dog) requires physical confinement that holds the dog safely and securely within physical walls, more than a rope tied to a stick in the ground or a battery-operated collar.

This issue grows even more complicated when the dog at the end of that chain or wearing that electronic collar is a Doberman Pinscher. As a Doberman owner, you are an ambassador for the breed in an age where insurance companies are known to deny home-owners coverage to owners of dogs of the Doberman's type, and vicious dog legislation targets specific breeds, such as Rottweilers, Pit Bulls, and, of course, Doberman Pinschers.

The "Vicious" Doberman

The vast majority of these dogs live as responsible canine citizens in the care of responsible owners, but it takes only one dog handled by an irresponsible owner to cast yet another black eye on a dog that hails from lines produced to protect human families and property. It's human nature: One bad experience with a Doberman, and all Dobermans must thus be unstable, vicious, and deserving of fear and exile. Ignorance is no excuse. Whether the cause of a mistake (or tragedy) is an owner's ego or a well-meaning blunder, the result is the same: possible injuries to children, adults, or other animals, permanent destruction of a dog's character and his relationship with his owner, a possible death sentence for the animal, and lawsuits.

Being an effective ambassador for this breed means training and socializing the dog diligently, caring for him properly, housing him safely and securely, supplying him with plenty of exercise to keep those sinewy muscles taut, and helping the general population see what amazing dogs Dobermans can be. It's a big job, a big responsibility. But the long-term benefits of living with such a loyal, intelligent, and dynamic animal are well worth the effort for the individual and the family that is up to the task.

KEEPING DOBERMANS GLEAMING

Even though they are short-haired dogs, Doberman Pinschers shed. The good news is that as a short-haired dog, the Doberman does not require a lot of grooming, but regular attention—not only to the coat, but also to the nails, teeth, and ears—is still necessary to keep the animal looking and feeling his best.

The Grooming Regimen

The best time to introduce the grooming regimen to your Doberman is while he is still a puppy. The animal is more impressionable at a young age (and more manageable), and is therefore more likely to tolerate your preening and probing. With proper handling and gentle training, many, if not most, dogs come to enjoy the various grooming procedures, viewing these sessions as special times when they receive full attention from their owners. If yours is one of those rare dogs that does not take kindly to being handled with such familiarity, be gentle but firm when introducing him to this vital regimen, keep the sessions short and positive in the beginning, and use praise and treats. Be patient, and in time, your

The well-groomed Doberman glistens in the sun and catches the eye of anyone lucky enough to pass by.

Doberman must (and will) learn to tolerate the regimen, and we hope even enjoy, your actions.

Brushing Basics

Brushing your Doberman regularly—if not every day, at least twice a week for 10 minutes or so each session—will help keep the dog's coat shining and his skin healthy. Besides loosening the dandruff and stimulating blood circulation, brushing also removes loose hair that may be trapped in the coat, while at the same time distributing the skin oils that make the coat shine.

Introduce your Doberman to the brushing routine right away, and use a moderately stiff brush, available at any pet supply store. Brush the dog gently, but make sure you go all the way down to the skin, brushing in the direction of the coat's growth. Use a comb to work out the occasional mat.

Keep the sessions short, and make sure that over time you brush every part of the dog's body. Brushing can actually be a valuable training tool, in that it reinforces for the dog that you are the boss and he must cooperate physically with your requests. Brushing sessions also provide you with the opportunity to inspect your dog for potential health problems. Check the paws for burrs, the ears for foxtails, the skin for lumps and bumps; you may catch a budding problem in its earliest stages, while your dog learns to tolerate your touch on such sensitive areas as his paws and ears.

Bathing

Every now and then every Doberman needs a bath. You won't need a calendar to figure out when this might be; your nose will tell you.

Most pet owners don't have their own in-home professional canine bathtub, so many use their own bathtubs in which to wash their dogs. (The smart ones also make sure to place a rubber mat on the tub floor, both to protect the finish and to offer the dog stable footing.) There is nothing wrong with this idea, as you can clean the tub afterward, but if you would rather not share your tub with your dog, you do have other options. You can install a special tub in your garage or basement, or, weather permitting, bathe your dog outdoors in a tub or with a hose while you keep him restrained on a leash.

Whichever bathing system you choose, the procedure is essentially the same:

1. First, wet the Doberman's coat down to the skin with water that is neither too hot nor too cold.

Rinse the dog thoroughly of shampoo during the bath, and dry her thoroughly afterward to keep her skin and coat healthy and clear.

2. Work in the shampoo and rinse the dog thoroughly. Then rinse the dog again; residual shampoo can dry the skin.

3. Be careful not to get shampoo in your pet's eyes and prevent irritation or infection.

4. If you are working indoors, you'll want to "squeeze" excess water from your pet's coat immediately after rinsing, and be prepared to toss a towel over the animal before he can execute his traditional canine water-removing shake.

5. Leave your Doberman indoors until his coat dries completely, both as a health precaution and as insurance that the animal won't roll around in something unmentionable while his coat is still wet.

Professional Groomers

If you would rather not go through all this, you can, of course, have a professional groomer bathe your dog. Not only can you expect to get a thorough, first-rate job (if you don't, find another groomer), but groomers are often the first to notice that a dog has an ear infection, a skin disorder, or another ailment that requires a veterinarian's care. A groomer can also be your best source of information for recommendations about grooming maintenance at home.

To find a good groomer, ask breeders, veterinarians, and fellow dog owners in your area for referrals, and choose a groomer with a clean shop, who has a good rapport with canine clients, and whose finished products you admire.

The Doberman is relatively easy to groom, but grooming must be done regularly by either the owner or a professional groomer.

Cleaning the Ears

Whether your Doberman sports natural ears or the cropped version, those ears require diligent attention. Cropped ears permit more air circulation than flopped natural ears do, but every ear, cropped and natural alike, must be tended to both inside and out.

Clean the ear flaps every few weeks or so with a damp cloth or a towel soaked in mineral oil. Never probe into the ear canal with a cotton swab or similar item, as this can injure the delicate recesses of the ear. Slight accumulations of wax can be cleared with a solution

Some Dobermans have excessive hair growth in their ear canals, which can contribute to infections. If your dog is one of these, your veterinarian may recommend that some of the hairs be plucked to improve air circulation. You can even do this yourself: Using tweezers, carefully remove those hair shafts that come out with minimum effort.

The Anal Sacs

Another potential grooming concern involves the anal sacs, the pungent contents of which are used to mark territory. Typically, the substance is released during normal defecation, but it may also be discharged when the dog is frightened or involved in a fight.

Sometimes a dog's anal sacs can become clogged, causing the glands within to enlarge, which in turn causes discomfort for the dog. Typically, the dog will drag his rear end on the ground in an attempt to alleviate the condition; he will also resort to frequent licking of the troubled area.

To prevent infection, the glands must be emptied. You can have your veterinarian or even your groomer do this for you, but if your dog seems to have a chronic anal sac problem, you might want to learn to do it yourself. It's a fairly simple task, but it requires a certain level of precision. It is not wise, however, to empty the sacs routinely if your dog does not have a problem. Most dogs never require attention to the anal sacs, thanks to a proper diet and regu-

that can be obtained from your veterinarian, but if you notice a heavy accumulation of wax inside the ear canal, let your veterinarian handle the situation.

Cropped ears promote better ear circulation, which is less likely to lead to infection; however, both natural and cropped ears require regular evaluation and cleaning.

Even though they are a short-haired breed, Dobermans do shed.

lar healthy elimination habits. Unnecessary routine "treatment" can lead to a chronic problem that would otherwise not have occurred.

Tough Stains and Odors

Doberman Pinschers are active, curious dogs, and sometimes this can lead to particularly messy situations that require special attention.

For tough grooming challenges, such as the removal of paint, tree sap, tar, or similar substances from the dog's coat, soak the affected area with mineral or vegetable oil for 24 hours, then try washing the area with soap and water. Despite what well-meaning "experts" may tell you, it is best *not* to use kerosene, turpentine, or the like on your pet, as these can be harmful and even poisonous to the animal, inside and out. One exception may be the use of rubbing alcohol to remove tree sap from the coat. If you do attempt this, keep the alcohol away from the dog's eyes, nose, and any open sores he may have. Remember, too, that sometimes the most humane remedy is simply to remove the offending material as well as the hair it clings to with scissors or electric clippers. The hair will grow back.

If your pet should ever have the misfortune of encountering a skunk, the only proven remedy is good old soap and water. Wash the dog thoroughly after such an encounter—twice if necessary—and let time and fresh air take their course. With luck, in a day or two the experience should be nothing but a bad memory. Rumor has it that rinsing the dog with tomato juice can help to neutralize the smell, and it

won't hurt the dog. Diluted lemon juice has also been credited as a remedy, but this can sting the dog's skin and eyes.

Of course no dog is odorless, and you will quickly learn to recognize the normal healthy scent of your pet. Should that scent change, you'll know something might be wrong. A particularly foul odor around your dog's neck area, for example, could be a sign of an ear infection or dental problem, in which case veterinary attention is called for. Or it could simply mean that it's time to clean or replace the dog's collar.

Pay close attention to any major changes to your Doberman's typical scent—it can be a sign of infection.

The stunning Doberman appearance occurs not by accident, but by a magical combination of routine grooming, emotional stimulation, and regular exercise.

Proper care of teeth and nails plays an important role in maintaining your pet's overall health and comfort.

Nail Trimming

Most Dobermans require nail trimming every two months or so. Some owners feel a little squeamish about doing this themselves, but it's really a rather simple procedure—and painless for the animal if done correctly. First gather the right tools: a special nail clipper designed for large dogs, a pet nail file, and a styptic pencil or powder to stop bleeding, all of which are available from pet supply stores.

Use well-made nail clippers designed specifically for the thick nails of large dogs.

The quick: What you want to trim from the nail is the "hook," the tip of the nail that curves downward. If you trim any higher than this, you risk cutting into the "quick" of the nail, the vein that runs through most of the nail, and that can bleed profusely when severed. The quick is visible to the naked eye on most light-colored dogs. Dark nails, such as those of the Doberman, provide more of a challenge. You can usually spot the quick area of a dark nail by illuminating the nail with the beam of a flashlight; the quick will appear darker in front of the light than will the tip. If you remain nervous about this, clip the nails more frequently and trim just the very tip to avoid any risk.

Accidents do happen, of course, and it's not unlikely that you may clip too deeply, or "quick," the nail. Don't panic. This may be messy, but it's not a major incident. Apply the stypic pencil or blood-stop powder, which you have nearby, and the bleeding will stop.

If the previous scenario bothers you, you might consider filing the nails down instead. Of course this can take longer and may be even more

uncomfortable for the dog. A better option might be simply to have your groomer or your veterinarian do the job.

Unclipped nails: So why bother clipping nails in the first place? The answer is simple. Unclipped nails can deform your Doberman's feet, permanently affecting his stance and gait. There is also the chance that a long nail can snag on something and break a toe, or the nail could break off entirely. The dog can recover from such an injury, but he will suffer needless pain—and all because of your inattention. A better option is to inspect your pet's nails regularly, trim them when necessary, and if you really want to stay ahead of the game, take your Doberman for lots of long walks as walking helps to keep the nails trim.

Dental Care

Part of your responsibility in caring for your Doberman is regularly inspecting your pet's teeth, but sometimes even without an inspection you figure out that something may be wrong. Does the animal have bad breath? That is usually the first sign that there is a gum or tooth problem of some kind.

Gum problems: Gum problems are more common in older dogs, but puppies as young as nine months of age have been known to require professional teeth cleaning because deposits of calculus and tartar have formed on their teeth and gums. Calculus is a stonelike material that accumulates on teeth, acting like a splinter under the gums. Infection often follows, eventually leading to bone and tooth loss. Frequently, this occurs without any noticeable signs other than bad breath and/or red or bleeding gums.

Stains: Yellow stains on the teeth can be caused by plaque, which is constantly forming on the tooth surface. Soft, sticky foods are said to contribute to plaque formation, just as hard foods, such as kibble and biscuits, help scrape plaque off of the teeth. Plaque will form regardless of diet, however, eventually calcifying and turning into calculus.

Brushing the teeth: To deal with this problem, veterinarians recommend routine cleaning of a dog's teeth, both professionally and at home. You can (and should) "brush" your dog's teeth in various ways. One method involves wrapping a thin washcloth or a piece of gauze around your index finger and using it as a toothbrush, rubbing the teeth and gums with a back-and-forth or circular motion. Another option is to use a toothbrush that is designed for dogs.

If your pet needs some coaxing to cooperate with this strange procedure, you can fortify the material or the toothbrush with a dab of toothpaste that is formulated especially for dogs in flavors that appeal to the canine

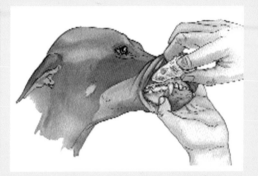

Brush your Doberman's teeth with either a piece of gauze or a toothbrush designed for the canine mouth and teeth.

palate. You must *never*, however, use "human" toothpaste on a dog's teeth, as the detergents in such products are too strong for the canine digestive system.

Introduce tooth brushing to your Doberman when he is still a puppy, and be careful not to upset or frighten him. If you upset the youngster, he may forever resist you in all future attempts. Keep the sessions brief, be generous with the praise and treats, and use a little flavoring if it helps. Once you're in the routine, clean your dog's teeth several times a week.

Professional Cleaning

Supplement your routine home care of your dog's teeth with professional cleanings done by your veterinarian once or twice a year. The more diligent you are helping to remove plaque from your dog's teeth at home, the less likely your dog will develop serious gum disease later in his life, and the more likely he will keep his teeth well into old age.

FOOD AND FITNESS

Your Doberman's overall well-being will be determined largely by both the quantity and the quality of the food you provide him. Simply put, whether your pet will be healthy or sickly, irritable or content, well behaved or mischievous will depend a great deal on his regular daily diet.

A poor diet can actually reduce your dog's life span, or at least deplete the animal's spirit and energy, compromising his quality of life. A dog that enjoys a well-balanced diet, on the other hand, is more likely to achieve and maintain his full genetic potential and enjoy increased stamina, a more positive mental disposition, and even an improved appearance, most evident in the condition of his coat. The latter, of course, is the most obvious indicator of a dog's general state of health. A shiny, thick coat is a sign of nutritional vitality, while a dull, uneven coat is your first clue that something may be wrong.

The Function of Nutrients

Before making an intelligent, informed decision about what to feed your Doberman, it is helpful to understand the basic function of nutrients, the chemical components needed for

A proper diet helps the Doberman Pinscher maintain what the breed's ardent fans refer to as "the look of eagles."

optimal growth, body maintenance, physical energy, and reproduction: proteins, carbohydrates, fats, vitamins, minerals, and water.

Protein

The most practical and useful source of high-quality protein for dogs is meat, although meat quality can vary. A major consideration in the development of a dog's feeding program, therefore, should be the quality and ease of assimilation of the protein the diet provides, because many of the essential amino acids available in meats cannot be synthesized by dogs. If there is a deficiency in one or more of these amino acids, the animal's body will automatically distribute those available to the most vital life functions first, depriving skin, coat, and bones of proper nutrition.

Carbohydrates

While being a vital source of energy, in their raw form carbohydrates cannot be fully assimilated by dogs. If raw or improperly cooked, they can actually undermine a good feeding program,

having a tendency to ferment in the animal's intestines. When processed in the manufacturing of dog food, then, these compounds must be converted to a usable form. The source and preparation of carbohydrates are therefore the most important factors in their digestibility. It is important that fiber—a complex chemical form of carbohydrates—be available as well, to facilitate optimum digestion.

Fats

With an energy concentration more than twice that of protein or carbohydrates, fats are crucial in providing energy to fuel body processes. They also supply essential fatty acids

A balance of high-quality nutrients is the key to the optimum Doberman diet.

necessary for overall health. Pure, high-quality lard and poultry fat are excellent fat sources because they are easily absorbed and good tasting. Fats must occur in controlled amounts, of course, to prevent obesity.

Vitamins and Minerals

Vitamins are components of, and catalysts for, the body's enzyme systems. They also maintain a balance between constructive and destructive cell changes, helping dogs resist disease and infection.

There are at least 14 minerals essential for life, and these have several functions in a dog's body. Elements of teeth and bone, minerals also regulate body fluids and serve as catalysts for the body's chemical reactions. Like many nutrients, minerals are required only in small quantities; excesses and imbalances can actually be dangerous to your dog. Moreover, in creating a balanced diet, it's not enough that all the nutrients are present; it's the proportion and order of these nutrients in the food that is critical. It is thus usually not wise to haphazardly offer supplements to a dog that is receiving a healthy, well-balanced diet; you might throw that diet out of balance.

Water

Water, too, is a nutrient, perhaps the most important nutrient in that it is vital to every cell, every organ, every system for proper functioning. You must never take for granted your responsibility of supplying your pet with a constant supply of fresh, clean water at all times. Remember, too, that even in frigid temperatures, dogs need their water!

Commercial Dog Food

While there are those courageous dog owners who prepare home-cooked diets for their pets, and who study the issue at a Ph.D. level to ensure that they are properly nourishing them, the vast majority of people depend on commercial manufacturers to provide their pets' diets. Unfortunately, though, not all com-

Don't let the endless choices confuse you: Most high-quality commercial dog foods will keep a Doberman healthy and beautiful.

TIP

Generic Brands

The foods to avoid are the obscure, so-called "bargain" or generic brands, which are more likely to contain inferior and even harmful ingredients. Many are produced with little or no analysis, resulting in nutritional deficiencies that can contribute to skin and coat problems, and to digestive and intestinal disorders.

mercial diets are created equal, and you must choose well to ensure that your dog receives its optimum nutrition.

It's sad enough that consumer preferences in choosing dog food are more likely to be determined by price than on what a food offers a dog nutritionally. What makes the situation worse is the fact that many commercial dog food packages claim *complete nutrition,* but contain nutrients that never nourish the dog because the animal's system cannot digest and absorb them.

It is not the purpose of this book to recommend a particular brand of dog food for your Doberman. There are many high-quality foods manufactured commercially that would do justice to almost any dog's feeding program. Nevertheless, you aren't likely to go wrong if you buy one of the so-called "premium" brands available in most pet supply stores. Most of these foods are high-caliber, nutritionally balanced diets representing the best knowledge we have about animal nutrition. You may, however, want to read the sales literature for different brands before making your selection.

While generally not as sophisticated as the specialty brands found in pet supply stores, many supermarket brands, especially the well-known national brands, do provide the minimal daily nutritional requirements to keep a dog in decent health. Before choosing one of these on price alone, however, remember that quite often a dog must eat more of

these foods to receive the same nutritional benefits he might receive from the premium foods.

There is, in fact, solid clinical proof that there is a nutritional difference between the higher-quality dog foods that claim to be "complete and balanced" and the bargain and generic brands. Studies have illustrated these differences, both in the negative, possibly dangerous, effects the low-end foods have on dogs, and whether various foods meet national standards or even their own guaranteed label analyses. These studies have left no doubt that the greatest distinction between bargain brands and their more expensive, higher-quality competitors is not price at all; it's nutrition. Put simply, one gets what one pays for.

Types of Commercial Dog Food

Once you have decided to feed your Doberman a high-quality commercial food, just how do you choose which one?

There are essentially three basic types of dog food: canned, dry, and semi-moist. The benefits of most commercial diets is that they are supposed to be complete and balanced and meet all of a dog's nutritional needs. As we have seen, however, you must choose wisely, preferably only those foods that meet the standards and protocols issued by the Association of American

To help ensure a healthy future for your pet, teach your puppy that he is to eat only his *food (not yours) out of* his *food dishes (not yours).*

Offer your Doberman food from your plate or dinner table, and you threaten to undermine the legendary beauty of this dog by promoting weight gain and undermining the beautiful sheen of her coat.

Feed Control Officials (foods that do will carry the AAFCO seal). Though price should not be your only guide, there are high-quality foods in all price ranges that meet this goal.

Canned food: Canned food typically contains all the necessary nutrients a dog needs: meats, grains, and added vitamins and minerals. Canned foods are soft foods, so if they comprise a dog's entire diet, they won't facilitate dental health, and they tend to produce looser stools. They are, however, quite palatable, and many owners use them as flavoring for a diet dominated by dry kibble.

Dry food: Odds are if you were to ask breeders and veterinarians what they would recommend for the canine diet, most would give the nod to dry kibble. Dry foods contain (or at least should contain) the same basic contents as those you find in canned foods, except that the moisture content has been reduced or eliminated during the manufacturing process. A dog eating these types of foods makes up for the loss of moisture by drinking more water. High-quality versions of these foods are convenient, clean, and nutritionally complete, and they produce smaller, firmer stools.

Semimoist food: Also expected to be nutritionally complete (if, of course, produced by a reliable manufacturer), semimoist foods boast a moisture content that lies somewhere between that of dry and canned foods. Typically lauded for their convenience, these foods are often packaged as individual servings, yet they may

also contain artificial coloring agents that are unnecessary in the canine diet. Again, many owners prefer using these as flavoring rather than as the bulk of their pets' diets.

Special Diets

Years ago not much was known about the canine diet. Thanks to researchers who have served both veterinary science and the major dog food manufacturers, we learn more every day about what makes up the optimum canine diet. This has been taken even further in the last few decades with the development of specialized canine diets.

It began with the development of foods designed for puppies, as growing puppies require more nutrients and energy than their parents do. Canine athletes and working dogs now also have their own formulations to supply their extraordinary energy needs, as do pregnant and lactating moms. We also find foods that are low in calories and fat, designed both to help a dog lose excess pounds and to prevent a dog, typically an aging one, from putting on those excess pounds as he slows down. Older dogs may also benefit from low-protein foods that prevent strain on the dog's aging organs. Your veterinarian might even recommend one of the many so-called prescription diets (available only from veterinarians) that target specific health problems in dogs, such as diabetes or urinary tract problems, or foods designed to help keep a dog's teeth healthy.

Dogs are living longer now than they did when they were simply thrown a slab of leftover meat from the table and a piece of bread, thanks to the pet-food revolution. It is, however, wise to consult your dog's veterinarian should you be considering a special diet for your dog. Together you may decide that your beloved Doberman really doesn't require the diet of a working sled dog, or that your healthy eight-year-old companion might be ready to switch over to a diet for aging dogs to ensure that his condition continues.

How to Feed

As with choosing the food for your dog, so must you make choices on how to feed your dog that food.

Take a look at the ideal Doberman: a sleek and beautiful dog with muscles that seem to radiate beneath that shining coat. Now imagine a Doberman whose muscles you cannot see so defined beneath a coat that is dull and chalky, a sad and lifeless Doberman encumbered by an overall bloat. Both images reveal how important a healthy and properly offered diet is to that ideal Doberman profile.

Table Foods

The Doberman is meant to view the world with "the look of eagles" and to impart the aura of an athlete as he walks down the street. Diet is an important key. Unfortunately, though, there are well-meaning dog owners among us who just can't help but share their own food with their dogs. They cannot resist the sad-eyed look of a Doberman begging at the table, and they figure that as long as the food is healthy—eggs, cottage cheese, some leftover steak—what harm can it do? Plenty, if the dog is receiving a complete and balanced commercial food that will only be thrown off balance by the addition of unnecessary nutrients.

Most owners are not sufficiently trained to properly supplement a complete commercially produced canine diet with so-called table foods. Many also believe that like humans, dogs crave a change in tastes and flavors in their diets. Both of these philosophies can lead to an unhealthy and overweight Doberman Pinscher, not to mention one that also becomes a very picky eater. Teach your dog that *your* food is not the dog's food, that he is to rely solely upon his own rations for sustenance, and you take an important step toward lengthening your pet's life span and enhancing its quality.

An overweight Doberman is a very sad and uncomfortable Doberman. Keep your dog fit, on the other hand, and you will probably extend both the length and quality of his life.

Go ahead and change your dog's diet as his age and condition evolves, perhaps even spike the food with a bit of flavoring such as a spoonful of canned dog food mixed with the kibble, and offer the dog treats in training and for good behavior (preferably treats designed for dogs). All a dog requires nutritionally is not variety, but a healthy, well-balanced diet. You have the power to supply that, and to instruct family members and friends that they are not to interfere by slipping the dog table scraps or offering him sweets and French fries when you're not looking.

How Often to Feed

How often you feed your dog usually revolves around your schedule and the dog's age, but there are several important qualifications:

✔ Until they are 12 weeks of age puppies should be fed four times a day. Their stomachs are small, plus they need the extra nourishment to fuel the tremendous growth they experience during these critical weeks.

✔ Likewise, from three to six months of age, a program of three meals a day is ideal.

✔ After six months, two meals a day will usually suffice until the animal reaches his first birthday, at which time you may decide to switch to a once-a-day feeding schedule if that is most convenient for you.

Many pet owners prefer, however, to remain on a twice-a-day feeding schedule, dividing their dog's daily ration into two halves. This is probably better for the dog's digestion and may be more satisfying. In addition to alleviating hunger pangs that may plague a dog fed once a day, smaller meals can help to prevent the onset of the deadly condition known as *canine bloat* (more on this condition in the chapter on Doberman health). Pet owners who still prefer a once-a-day program can minimize begging behavior and hunger pangs by giving their dogs a biscuit or two during family mealtimes.

Doberman Obesity

Whichever dietary regimen you adopt, the most important consideration is that you don't overfeed your dog. Stick to the routine; evaluate any changes in your pet's energy requirements, age, or health that may require a change in diet or feeding practices; and be mindful of your Doberman's general appearance.

As this Doberman with a talent for agility trials demonstrates, this naturally athletic breed requires and thrives on regular, age-appropriate exercise from puppyhood to old age.

people, are individuals. Two Dobermans of the same size and activity range might very well need different amounts of food simply because of varying metabolisms.

The Importance of Exercise

A nutritionally complete diet is a great foundation for health, but it won't keep your pet's muscles toned. If you want to keep a Doberman in top physical condition you'll have to make sure he gets plenty of exercise, which, you will find, is good for the dog's psyche, as well.

Most dogs, particularly active, robust dogs like the Doberman, need about an hour of physical activity each day to keep them fit and content. Exercises suited to the Doberman's talents include swimming, agility, and running and jogging. (Check things out with the dog's veterinarian ahead of time, just to make sure the animal is up to the sport at hand, work gradually to build your dog's condition over time, and avoid working during the highest heat of the day.)

Water exercise: While Doberman Pinschers are not classic "water dogs," they can be taught to enjoy the water. If you don't happen to have your own swimming pool in the backyard, the most practical way to get your dog to swim is simply to have him retrieve objects from a lake or other suitable body of water. Avoid water that is polluted, dangerously cold, excessively turbulent, or that does not provide easy access to the shore. If you live near the ocean and

If the dog seems to be gaining weight (you find you cannot easily feel the contours of his ribs beneath your fingers as you run your hands over his rib cage), reduce your pet's food intake or switch to a food designed for weight reduction, and by all means, kick up the dog's exercise. If, on the other hand, the ribs beneath your fingers feel a little too sharp and defined to the touch and you fear your dog may be getting too thin, you may need to increase the daily ration. In either case, it is wise to consult your dog's veterinarian before you make any radical dietary adjustments. Weight loss or weight gain can be signs of illness, so it is best to rule out such problems before assuming that all that is required is a change in diet or exercise.

Note that pregnant or lactating moms, dogs with rigorous work regimens, or dogs that spend a good deal of time outdoors in cold weather will require greater amounts of food than is prescribed for those dogs leading more normal lives. Remember, too, that dogs, like

your dog is a good swimmer, he may enjoy running through the waves, but in the interest of PR (Public Relations), avoid beaches where dogs are not allowed, and stay away from peak times when the beaches are crowded with people who might fear your Doberman.

Agility: If your dog enjoys leaping and jumping and traversing obstacles, he may be a candidate for the popular canine sport of agility. Here, with exuberant coaching from their owners, dogs of all shapes and sizes traverse a maze of jumps and tunnels and all manner of obstacles. Fun and challenging, agility contributes to a dog's overall training, and also provides him with ample activity in a controlled situation.

Running: Running is a great Doberman exercise, but only under constant supervision. A beautifully behaved Doberman whose owner has access to a big open field or park might be able to get away with working the dog off-leash, but a safer, more politically correct alternative might be visiting a dog park, where well-trained dogs are invited to run and play off-leash in a confined area with other well-trained dogs.

Formal jogging: And finally, if you would like to try formal jogging with your Doberman, remember that puppies and older dogs are not suited to this activity, and even healthy dogs in their prime should not be run for more than a couple of miles. Human runners who experience occasional pain or discomfort know enough to stop and rest or quit for the day; a dog running with his owner, however, can't or possibly won't communicate physical difficulties he may be experiencing.

Setting a good exercise regimen for your puppy will set a foundation for his lifelong health.

Exercise and Aging

Puppies get all the exercise they need just being puppies. Older dogs, however, have special needs. The older guys are, for instance, less resistant to wet and cold weather. For some dogs, that means providing the animal with a coat or sweater, or at least a thorough drying if you are caught with him in a downpour.

An older Doberman, though still typically an active dog into old age, may prefer and require a slower pace. Some dogs go through life running and playing with the kids in the family, activity that keeps them fit and healthy for years. But times and bodies change, so don't be surprised if some day the dog shuns the advances of puppies and children—and don't force the issue. Rescue your aging pet if you see that he is getting annoyed with youngsters, and provide him with a secluded spot where he can retreat and rest without unwanted attention. Even an older dog, though, will want and need daily walks and time spent with the family, which will keep the animal content and fit.

TRAINING YOUR DOBERMAN

Training your Doberman is crucial to the quality of the relationship the animal will develop with you and your family. A pet that constantly misbehaves becomes a source of escalating frustration, inevitably compromising his status as a valued member of the household and of society.

Unruly and vicious dogs that go so far as to attack innocent people and/or other animals can cause endless grief for all concerned, their owners subjected to costly lawsuits. More often than not, the root of the problem turns out to be improper handling and careless or insufficient training. Training, then, is an important preventive measure for a dog's well-being and survival, but there is a right way—and many wrong ways—to go about it.

Philosophies

Dogs are more content and secure when they live according to discipline and boundaries. The headstrong among them may chal-

Let's be honest—if you ignore the Doberman's need for socialization and training, you will create a monster.

lenge their owners for authority, but they will also obey and cooperate willingly once they learn who is the boss. Humane and effective training of a Doberman is no different from training any dog. You begin with socializing the dog to as many people, children, and other dogs as possible at the earliest age. Keep the sessions short and positive—and don't forget the treat rewards—and the dog will learn how nice it is to be a part of society.

Puppy kindergarten classes: Formal training can actually begin at about 12 weeks of age with so-called puppy kindergarten classes. Here, young puppies can play with each other (hence promoting their socialization to other dogs) and begin to learn basic commands that are taught in ways that engage their young-puppy views of the world. A puppy that has been through this process is then far more prepared to take on the rigors of more structured training as he matures.

Trainers: Which brings us to the subject of training classes and professional trainers. Far too many dog owners believe they don't need help from a professional. The many dogs that end up in animal shelters because of "behavior problems" are evidence that too often this isn't the case.

You can find good trainers conducting classes through community recreation departments, through their own private practices or local dog clubs, and even at pet supply stores and veterinary hospitals. Find a trainer who understands and respects the Doberman breed, who employs methods of positive reinforcement (a good trainer does not require harsh training collars or negative, heavy-handed training techniques), and who is skilled in working with potentially headstrong dogs (not all trainers are). The best-kept secret among the best trainers is that in teaching their canine students, they are also teaching the humans on the other end of the leash. People are not born knowing how to train and communicate with dogs, so both parties need to learn.

One of the most important lessons that everyone involved must learn is that training never ends. You and your Doberman may graduate with honors from training class, but that is only the beginning. You must constantly practice and reinforce what you have learned for the rest of the dog's life to ensure that your dog remains a well-behaved citizen.

Repetition Is the Key

Training consists of establishing a series of conditioned reflexes in your pet. The way to do this is through repetition. The degree to which you are successful here depends as much on the animal's attention and concentration as it does on your own enthusiasm. That's why it is best to keep beginning training sessions brief, no more than 10 to 15 minutes at a time.

Name: A logical first step is to teach the animal his name, whether the student is a puppy or an adult dog that may have had another name in his former life. Continuous use of the dog's name when you address your pet—repetition—will get the concept across quickly.

Come: Teaching your puppy or dog to come to you on command is another lesson you can work on as soon as the animal joins the household. Begin by coaxing the animal with your voice. It may help to squat down to the dog's eye level and reach out your hand to communicate the message. In most cases, the dog will respond to such devices, even if it's purely out of instinct. Eventually, with practice and a positive attitude on your part, the dog will understand what *"Come"* means when you say it, reacting accordingly.

Of course at some point, your pet may test your will by not responding to your command to come to you. This is especially common

---

TIP

Punishing Your Dog

It does no good to punish your dog by withholding food, water, shelter, or other basic necessities. Aside from being useless, cruel, and reprehensible, this serves no useful purpose in the training process and can lead to even bigger problems.

Stick religiously to the routine, and you will be amazed at how quickly your puppy can master the fine art of house-training.

during the period of canine adolescence at about six months of age or so. Do not let such a challenge to your authority, however insignif-icant it may seem, go unnoticed. This only serves to reinforce to the animal that he can disregard you and have his way when he wants to—an undesirable precedent, to be sure, espe-cially when you consider that the command may some day keep the dog out of danger.

Dealing with Disobedience

It is your job to teach your dog that you are the boss, or alpha, and this may not happen overnight. If your pet chooses to disobey you, use your tone of voice to communicate your displeasure. Do so immediately, as dogs have a short attention span and will not understand what they are being scolded for if you wait too long after the fact.

Never use violence, or even the threat of it, to mold a dog's behavior. Animals so condi-tioned can develop vicious tendencies, or become timid, cowering at their owner's every move. Neither behavior is desirable, and both can be difficult to correct—so put away the rolled-up newspapers! The only time you should even considering striking your dog is if he is threatening to bite you or someone else, and then of course, you have a major problem on your hands that even a skilled behaviorist may not be able to remedy.

Praise Gets Results

You will get the best results training your Doberman with lots of praise given lovingly and generously whenever the dog does something right. Your pet will then be far more inclined to respond favorably to future training efforts.

To maintain this productive arrangement, avoid calling your pet when you want to reprimand him for some improper behavior. If the dog believes he is being summoned for punishment—say, after he has an accident on the carpet—he will not be all that interested in coming when you call. When the dog does come, praise him. Always. If you need to reprimand or correct the dog, approach him to voice your complaint, the logic being that the dog should always associate coming to you as a positive, rewarding experience.

In spite of your best efforts, you are bound to experience setbacks during the training process, especially in the beginning. Be patient with your pet, and be consistent in your leadership. For example, if you do not want your dog to climb on the furniture or stand around the dinner table begging for handouts, don't make an exception just because you have guests in the house. Allowing "special" circumstances that negate whatever rules of conduct you are trying to establish is counterproductive.

Sooner or later, you will probably discover that your Doberman responds to commands with more vigor and enthusiasm when you are dangling a piece of food or a dog treat before his eyes. This is an acceptable form of reward, but don't overdo it. Your pet must learn to respond to you, not to a promised piece of cheese.

Saying "No"

Another basic command you will probably introduce early on is *"No!"* With a puppy in the house, you'll have plenty of opportunities to practice the word as the youngster explores both his new home and the limits of your own tolerance. Say *"No!"* with authority, say it only in response to valid circumstances, and say it loudly and sharply enough to communicate the urgency of your message, but without anger or emotion.

The earlier you introduce your puppy to such procedures as nail trimming, bathing, ear cleaning and toothbrushing, the more cooperative she will be in the future with professional groomers, veterinarians, and dog show judges.

It is also most effective to follow up the verbal reprimand with some kind of corrective action that will help your dog understand what he did wrong. For example, if the animal is chewing on a shoe, snatch the shoe away and replace it with an acceptable chew toy. In addition, don't leave shoes around on the floor where the puppy can find them, and tell the kids that if they leave their favorite toys or books on the floor, the puppy really can't be blamed for deciding those items must be fair game.

House-training

Your most urgent initial training goal will be to house-train your new pet. With luck, an adopted older dog will already be trained and simply require a refresher course on the protocols of his new home, but most puppies are new to the game. There are two basic methods of accomplishing this objective, depending primarily on your living situation. If you own a home, you can either paper-train your puppy indoors first, waiting until he has grown a bit before introducing him to the practice of doing his business outdoors, or you can skip paper-training, concentrating on the outdoors approach from the outset. Neither method is foolproof or accident-free.

If you're a condo or apartment dweller, you may not have such easy access to the outside, in which case you probably have no choice but to paper-train your pet first, before making the transition to the outdoors. Typically, this occurs with improved bladder and bowel control at about four months of age.

For house-training purposes, restrict the puppy to a single room. You will figure out right away why you don't want to give your

TIP

"Mistakes"
✔ When a "mistake" occurs and you are there to witness it, chastise the animal with your voice, and move him immediately to the correct spot.
✔ *Do not ever rub the dog's face in the mess.* Such a reaction will only complicate the process.
✔ Backtrack a little and widen the spread of newspaper somewhat if you think you may have proceeded with training too quickly, but continue toward your ultimate goal.
✔ Should the misdeed occur while you are away, it will not do any good to scold the dog upon your return. By that time, the animal will have difficulty associating your displeasure with the action that prompted it—you will just have to wait until the next time.

puppy free access to the house until he has control of his bladder and an understanding of where he should eliminate. The kitchen for many seems the ideal space for house-training confinement, if only because there is usually no carpeting to worry about when the inevitable "accident" occurs, and also because that is usually where the backdoor is.

Before you restrict your Doberman to his initial living space, inspect the area carefully, removing or neutralizing any items that may harm him, or that can be damaged by him. Puppies are inclined to chew, climb, or paw at

CHECKLIST

Choke Collars

1 Begin by placing the collar on your pet in the proper position so it hangs loosely around the dog's neck.

2 Allow the dog to walk around with the collar on and get used to the collar's weight and feel.

3 After a day or two of this exercise, affix the leash to the collar and let the dog run around with that too.

4 Next, take hold of the leash and try walking the animal. Keep the dog on your left side as this is where he should walk for training, and make sure the collar is in the correct position where it loosens as soon as you release pressure on the leash. Apply as little pressure as possible to the choking mechanism during this introduction phase.

almost anything that attracts their attention. Get down on your puppy's level and remove any dangers you find in his home: sharp edges, electrical cords that can be gnawed, poisonous materials that could be ingested, furniture that can tip over, and any other potential pitfalls.

The Paper-training Phase

As a dog emerges from infancy, he will probably begin to relieve himself each time in the same general location of his living space. Once you have determined the approximate spot your pet seems to favor, you can begin to paper-train him. The idea is to remove small sections of the floor covering gradually, beginning with those areas farthest away from the animal's "drop zone," exposing an ever-increasing amount of bare floor. As long as the animal continues to direct his efforts to the area of his living space that is covered with newspaper, keep reducing the size of that area over a period of several weeks until it measures about 3 square feet (0.278 m). Give the dog lots of praise whenever he performs to expectations and hits the target. If you feel some additional prompting may be in order, leave a bit of previously soiled paper on top of each new arrangement of floor covering as a subtle reminder to the puppy.

Help your dog understand that when he eliminates in the right spot on the paper, he can come out of his confined space and join the family in another part of the house. This becomes the greatest reward. You must do this as soon as the puppy finishes his business, though, so the youngster equates his liberation with what he has just done on the newspaper.

Transition to the Great Outdoors

As your Doberman grows and acquires better control of his bodily functions, he will need to relieve himself less frequently. The most likely times will probably be after eating, sleeping, or playing. Now you can begin taking the animal outside, praising him profusely when he does his business there. Returning to the same location at the same basic times every day will enhance the chances of continued success.

A fully grown dog may need to "go out" as many as four times a day; younger dogs may need relief as often as every two or three hours. In addition to watching the clock, you will need to learn to recognize the warning

A Doberman who will sit and stay reliably is a joy to his owner, and an excellent example of what this breed can achieve in the right hands.

signals that mean your pet is ready to do his duty. The dog may start sniffing at corners and turning around in circles or barking at the back door. Grab your coat and go!

Dog crate: During the transition stages of training, that is, when you remove the last of the dog's floor covering and begin to channel your pet's elimination habits outdoors, many trainers recommend confining the dog to an exercise pen, a particular room, or a dog crate at night or when you are not at home. Given the belief that a dog will not soil his "den," a dog crate is considered by many to be a handy tool for house-training as long as it is not abused. If you decide to house-train your dog with a crate, choose a crate that is large enough for the dog to walk in and turn around, pad the floor with comfortable blankets or pillows, and, with the exception of nighttime, do not confine the dog in the crate for long periods of time. With any kind of confinement, make sure to take the dog outside to relieve himself just before bedtime and as soon as possible in the morning.

The Direct Approach

Direct house-training, in which you skip the paper-training phase, still requires restricting the dog for the first few weeks with exercise pens, baby gates, or a dog crate, and perhaps even to an area carpeted with newspapers. The only difference is that you will try to anticipate your pet's need to relieve himself by taking him outside as often as possible during the course of each day, encouraging him from the start, perhaps even with an elimination command, to do his duty there.

The direct approach requires a little more effort on your part. To maximize the benefits of training, it's important that someone be available to accompany the dog outside with reasonable frequency, especially after playing, sleeping, or eating. Otherwise, the animal will have no choice but to relieve himself inside the home. As the weeks of training and positive reinforcement pass by, your dog's toilet habits will become fairly predictable, and your pet reliably house-trained.

Basic Training

At about six or seven months of age, your Doberman will be ready to proceed with more serious training. He may already have learned some basic commands working with you at home and perhaps in a puppy kindergarten class, but now you can step into more formal and structured training, either on your own or, ideally, with the help of a professional trainer privately or in a class situation.

In a class setting, you will not only have access to the knowledge and guidance of an expert, but such gatherings will also enhance your Doberman's socialization to other people and dogs. Keep in mind, though, that when all is said and done, the brunt of the responsibility of your dog's education rests squarely on you; in other words, you've got to do your homework. Remember, too, that while we will be exploring here one method for teaching the basic commands, you will no doubt find that there are a variety of methods that are both effective and humane.

Clicker training: You may find a trainer in your area who specializes in the increasingly popular method of clicker training. Considered by many to be an effective option for Dobermans, this is a purely positive method that involves clicking a small device every time the dog obeys a command.

Training with a Choke Collar

If you intend to train with a chain training collar, you can do so now. To use this on a puppy younger than six or seven months of age can lead to injury, as the youngster's neck muscles are not yet developed to withstand the effects of such collars. Despite their unflattering name, so-called "choke" collars are lauded by many trainers as valuable training tools,

provided they are used properly. The chain training collar will be a new sensation on the dog's neck, so gently allow the dog to grow accustomed to it in a positive manner. Do not, however, leave the collar on the dog as his everyday collar, as that can lead to injury.

With frequent practice and praise, the dog will learn to follow your movements at a pace and position that offer minimum resistance. At that point, whenever your Doberman begins to stray from your control, a quick, gentle tug on the leash will usually correct the behavior. Occasionally, a stronger response may be called for, but be careful not to hurt the dog by mis-using the device, applying the choke mechanism unrelentingly or with brutal force. In the wrong hands, a choke collar can indeed become an instrument of torture.

Note: Although you can begin increasing training periods to as long as half an hour as your dog matures, be sure to allow time for play whenever you go outside for training, too. Best done when "school" is out, playtime can serve as a reward for your dog's learning efforts and end the lesson on a pleasant, positive note.

Heel!

The next logical step is to teach the Doberman to heel on command. There is no quick and easy way to do this; it's simply a matter of repeating the motions until they become second nature and praising the dog whenever he performs to expectations.

With the dog positioned on your left side, start to walk forward, calling your Doberman's name, followed by the *heel* command, at the same time giving the leash a gentle tug to prompt the dog's movement. Continue moving forward. As the dog speeds up or falls behind,

Work with your puppy consistently from an early age—preferably with the help of a professional trainer—and you will begin to foster a dog that can blossom into the ideal Doberman Pinscher.

give the leash a light snap and repeat the *heel* command, praising the animal when he lines up with you again.

Limit practice sessions to no more than two a day. Eventually, you'll notice that your Doberman has begun to heel on command alone. Then you can start on more advanced maneuvering, such as 90- and 180-degree turns and other, more complicated drills. The ultimate test is to have your dog heel off-leash, but don't proceed to this level of training until the animal has fully mastered heeling on lead, and is reliably socialized to other people and dogs.

Sit!

In obedience training, dogs in the *heel* position are taught to sit automatically whenever their handlers stop walking. To teach this, walk the dog in the *heel* position, stop periodically, and give the *sit* command each time. Demonstrate the desired response by gently pushing your Doberman's rear down into a sitting posture, at the same time using your other hand to keep the animal's head up and facing forward.

Repeat this procedure continuously with the usual dose of praise, and before long, your pet will begin responding to your voice command alone. By that stage, you can ask the dog to sit virtually anytime, simply by voicing the command. Any lapse in performance can be easily corrected by repeating the command as you physically place the animal into position. With time, patience, consistency, and praise, you

won't even have to tell your Doberman to sit when the two of you come to a halt.

Stay!

Begin teaching *stay* with the dog in the *sit* position. Holding the leash in one hand, raise the palm of the other in front of the dog's face to signal the command as you say it. Having done so, step away from the animal as far as the leash allows, taking care not to exert any pressure on the leash that the dog may interpret as a signal to come forward. If your dog follows you anyway, offer a sharp *"No,"* and start over again.

After your pet has learned to respond to the *stay* command on the leash, see if he will follow the same instructions without it. Gradually increase both the distance you move away from the animal and the length of time you maintain the command until you can safely keep the dog in position for two or three minutes, even at a considerable distance.

Down!

Here, too, start with the dog in a sitting position. As you give the *down* command, ease the animal into a prone position, either by pushing down on his shoulders, lifting his front legs down and forward, or some combination of the two. Once the dog has assumed the correct position, hold your pet there for a moment, at the same time giving the *stay* command. Repeat the exercise several times during consecutive training sessions until the animal obeys you on voice command alone.

When your pet has learned the basic commands—*come, heel, sit, stay, down*—and can be relied upon to respond to each of them without fail or hesitation, preliminary training is complete. Certainly there is much more your Doberman can be taught, but with these initial hurdles

behind you, you can at least feel secure that the prescribed foundations have been established.

Dealing with Behavior Problems

Training is a lifelong endeavor, and in some cases, a necessity, especially when problems arise. Even after the essentials have been mastered, be prepared to deal with special behavior problems that may arise.

Excessive Barking

We can all appreciate a pet that promptly alerts us to the approach of strangers, and of course, most Doberman owners consider the bark to be part of the dog's protective qualities. But a dog that barks without end can become a terrible nuisance, both to you and to your neighbors. Whenever your Doberman gets out of hand in this area, give him a firm *"No"* and call the dog to you, demonstrating that there are definite limits to your tolerance of vocal bravado.

If the dog persists in his noisemaking, you might try confining him to a room, responding to any subsequent outbreaks by knocking loudly on the door and reprimanding him without actually entering the room, unless his vocalizations seem especially urgent and frenzied. What you want to avoid is giving the animal the false notion that you will come immediately every time he starts to "sing."

Praise can do wonders with any plan you come up with, such as arranging for friends to come to

Excessive barking can be a frustrating problem to remedy, but it must be addressed seriously if you are to avoid repeat visits from animal control officials.

the door so you can teach the dog to bark once or twice and then quiet down and come to you on command. Sometimes the answer is simply to increase the dog's daily exercise, as walking and running in the great outdoors are great stress relievers. If nothing seems to work, you may need to call in a qualified behaviorist for help. A skilled, humane, and objective expert can often better diagnose the cause of a problem and identify an effective remedy.

Jumping Up on People

The Doberman is not a dog that most people would like jumping up on them and knocking them down. If you have made the mistake of allowing your Doberman puppy to jump up on you to get attention, and you suddenly find that you have an adult Doberman that has made this behavior a habit, simply give the *down* command, which he is already familiar with, right? If the animal does not curtail the behavior, try raising your knee as the dog leaps up and gently knocking the animal off balance. After several such episodes, the dog will decide that this is not a practical way to greet you when you come home.

Climbing on Furniture

Here, too, prevention is best. If you don't want your adult Doberman to climb on the furniture, don't let the Doberman puppy do it either. If, however, it is too late for this, remember that repetitive commands and consistency can help. Tell the dog to get off the furniture again and again, and make sure the dog obeys and learns that he is not a welcome guest on beds and sofas.

If you discover that your dog sneaks onto furniture when you are away, you can place sheets of crackly paper (or a suitable substitute) on it; the sound should startle the dog and

deter him from doing it again. If that doesn't work, there is little alternative but to deny the dog access to those rooms when you are away.

Biting

Don't ever encourage your Doberman to bite, even in play, even when he is a young puppy. If the need arises, your dog will be protective enough; you don't need to teach him to be aggressive. If your dog does nip at you, even in play, voice your displeasure loudly, forcing the dog's jaws shut for several seconds. When the dog submits to your correction, praise him briefly and continue playing.

The number-one rule here is that no dog should ever intentionally bite a member of his family, and if this occurs you need to deal with the problem swiftly, seriously, and with the help of an expert. But remember, too, that you should never test the principle by teasing the dog, especially when he is eating or sleeping. Even the best-trained and well-behaved dogs have their limits.

Retrieving

Most dogs take to retrieving naturally, eagerly chasing down virtually anything you throw in their direction. Getting the object back, however, is not always so easy.

Whether you prefer to use *"Fetch"* or *"Get it,"* or some other choice of words, try to give the same command each time during retrieving exercises. Your Doberman will naturally tend to bring his prize back toward your general vicinity, if for no other reason than to have you continue the "game," but the dog may hesitate in relinquishing it. If that's the case, give the by-now-familiar commands to *sit* and *stay*, then approach the dog, taking the object from his mouth as you introduce a new command: *"Drop it"* or *"Let go."* If your student still resists, growling or turning away from you or holding on, give him a stern *"No"* to communicate your dissatisfaction. As always, performance will improve with practice and praise, and you will be confirming your position as boss.

Staying Alone

A more practical lesson you can teach your pet, preferably while he is still a puppy, is staying home alone. Some dogs left alone for the first time don't handle it very well; beset with anger or fear, they may bark and howl to the point of aggravating your neighbors, or they may tear through your home, destroying anything they can find.

You can help by occasionally isolating your Doberman for short but increasing periods of time in an area of your home where he cannot hear or see you—a spare room will suffice if you have one—but where you can still monitor any major disturbances that may occur. This will help the dog become acclimated to periods of solitude; it will also give you an insight into how much difficulty, if any, your pet is likely to give you in this area of behavior.

If your dog is barking because he just can't stand being away from his family, try leaving the house for a few minutes, and when the dog doesn't bark, run in and praise him. Leave again for a little longer period of time, and when the dog remains quiet again, praise him again. As preventive measures, make sure your dog gets plenty of exercise and attention every day, fashion a comfortable bed for him, when you leave provide water and perhaps a toy or a

treat or two, and secure the premises as best you can. See how your dog takes to this confinement and, of course, praise him heartily upon your "return."

Travel Training

You must also teach your Doberman how to behave when you want to take him along on vacation or even just to visit a friend across town. There are rules of conduct that apply here, but they are primarily meant for you, not the dog.

Most dogs love to stick their heads out of the windows of moving cars, but such behavior can be dangerous. Even if your Doberman does not fall out or be tempted to jump, there is still the possibility that the animal can sustain an eye injury or ear problem from prolonged exposure to high-velocity wind or foreign objects.

When traveling by car, it's best to keep your dog confined to a comfortable and properly sized cage or crate. If your car can't accommodate this, there are seat belt systems available for canine safety. If, heaven forbid, you are involved in an accident, such precautions improve the odds that the dog will escape serious injury.

The same rules apply for people who transport their pets in the back of pickup trucks. Never do so unless the dog is in a crate or attached to a specially designed harness. A standard leash is *not* sufficient to control the animal properly, and having no restraint at all is tantamount to criminal negligence. Many dogs have been killed as a result of such carelessness.

Finally, although you've probably heard it before, a few additional rules bear repeating. Try not to leave your Doberman in the car unattended, especially in warm weather when the rays and warmth of the sun can quickly turn the

Take advantage of your Doberman's natural talent for training by expanding your pet's horizons into such activities as advanced obedience trials, canine good citizenship, or agility.

car into a blazing oven, even if you park in the shade and leave the windows partially open. If you insist on bringing your dog with you, even on cooler days, make your absences as brief as possible and, when delayed, check on your pet with regular frequency. Better yet, if your travel involves the multiple starts and stops of errand-running, leave your pet at home.

Of course leaving the pet at home is an option when you travel on vacation, as well. While many people cringe at the thought of leaving a beloved pet at a boarding kennel, there are some fine facilities available run by people who genuinely love dogs. Leave your dog in the care of one of these, and you can enjoy your vacation without worry. Introduce your pet to boarding when he is a puppy, and you build a foundation that will come in handy for many years to come.

Advanced Training

If, during the course of your basic training efforts, you discover that both you and your Doberman develop a genuine zeal for such work, you might consider continuing your efforts on a higher plane of achievement.

For example, when the dog can *heel* both on and off its leash, and he will *come, sit, lie down, stay* on command, and stand for inspection by a judge, he can earn his "Companion Dog" title from the American Kennel Club. Another title awarded by the AKC is the Canine Good Citizen

title. To earn this the dog must show off his knowledge of basic obedience commands and exemplary socialization through such exercises as walking without pulling on the leash, allowing a stranger to pet and brush him, and showing that he is capable of ignoring distractions. Any obedience-rooted title enhances the reputations of both the individual dog and his breed. The more Dobermans are recognized officially as good citizens and obedience champions, the easier it is to convince the public that perhaps the image of this breed as an uncontrolled vicious monster is not all that accurate.

Another training venue in which Dobermans are common participants, though it is not required nor even highly recommended for family dogs, is that of guard dog training, culminating in official Schutzhund trials. If this is your goal—and remember, your Doberman will be a fine protector without it—working with a professional trainer is a *must*. The dog will have to learn to deal with simulated attacks, fleeing "criminals," and similar scenarios that are more appropriate for a dog doing police work than dealing with the challenges of family life.

HEALTHY AND HAPPY

Dogs are subject to a vast array of illnesses and injuries during the course of their lives. How we prevent and respond to these health problems can greatly influence both the animals' longevity and the overall quality of their lives.

The best advice is this: Know your Doberman—and your veterinarian. If you take a genuine interest in your pet, caring for him properly and making the extra effort to observe his movements, mannerisms, and temperament, and giving him a physical inspection now and then—you will be able to notice problems more quickly when they arise. This can mean the difference between life and death.

Recognizing Symptoms

It's not as important that you are able to diagnose a particular disease or the nature of an injury as it is that you recognize the symptoms. Most signs of trouble should be fairly obvious: fever, coughing, extreme loss or gain of appetite or weight, shivering, constipation,

A healthy Doberman does not come about by accident. She is the product of a sound breeding program, followed by an equally sound partnership between the dog's owner and veterinarian.

chronic diarrhea, abnormal stools, increased urination, labored breathing, lameness or paralysis, frequent vomiting, open wounds, hair loss, skin inflammations, unusual drooling or discharges, seizures, swollen joints or muscles, an awkward gait, bizarre behavior, loss of coordination, and obvious signs of pain.

Any one of these symptoms should prompt a phone call to your veterinarian, who will advise you of the best immediate course of action. The earlier a problem is noticed and treated, the better chance a dog has of survival.

Serious Diseases

What infectious diseases such as distemper, rabies, hepatitis, leptospirosis, parvovirus, and coronavirus have in common is that all can be prevented through routine vaccination. Puppies typically receive a series of four or five of the basic vaccines during their first few months of life, followed by boosters every year thereafter (the exception is rabies, which, in most areas, requires a booster every three years). These are

Current vaccines can protect puppies from a variety of serious canine ailments, such as parvovirus, distemper, and rabies.

Any person bitten by a dog suspected to be rabid must report the incident to a physician as soon as possible for treatment. Rabies is rare among dogs these days thanks to public health vaccine mandates, but even vaccinated dogs that bite are quarantined for a period of time determined by the dog's rabies vaccine status, just to be sure.

Parvovirus/Coronavirus

Carried in the feces of infected dogs, parvovirus typically attacks a dog's intestinal tract. Conquering this disease can be difficult, for the virus is a hardy one, capable of surviving under a wide range of temperatures and conditions. Furthermore, direct contact with an infected animal is not the only way the virus is transmitted. It can also be carried in the hair, feet, and feces of stricken animals, and even on a person's shoes and clothes.

Symptoms appearing within a week of exposure include fever, vomiting, bloody urine, and severe diarrhea (gray or yellow). Dehydration is swift, and death usually occurs within 72 hours if the dog is left untreated. Treatment includes supportive therapy carried out in a hospital to rehydrate the dog, but a positive outcome is not guaranteed. The virus is especially deadly to puppies, but whatever your Doberman's age, it is wise to keep him vaccinated and away from other dogs' wastes.

Coronavirus, which also attacks the intestines, does not tend to be as deadly as parvovirus, though its symptoms are basically identical. To be on the safe side, seek veteri-

not, of course, the only serious diseases and ailments that can affect dogs, as some conditions have genetic or environmental causes.

Rabies

Deadly to nonimmunized dogs and humans alike, the rabies virus enters the body through bite wounds inflicted by an infected animal. First, the stricken animal displays inexplicable mood swings, vacillating from irritability to affection. He also appears especially sensitive to noise and light, and it is not uncommon for rabid dogs to attempt to eat undigestable material such as wood or pieces of stone, all the while refusing normal food. In advanced stages, symptoms include attacking and biting, frenzied running, difficulty in swallowing, and uncontrollable drooling. During the final stages, the animal's body becomes completely paralyzed; convulsions and death soon follow.

nary attention the moment you suspect a problem to give the dog the best chance of making it through any serious illness.

Tetanus

Sometimes called lockjaw, tetanus is caused by poison-producing bacteria that thrive inside wounds where oxygen cannot penetrate. When a dog is seriously wounded, he should receive an antitetanus shot and follow-up treatment from the veterinarian. As another safety precaution, thoroughly clean and disinfect any wounds your Doberman may incur.

Tracheobronchitis

Dubbed "kennel cough" (much to the dismay of kennel operators), tracheobronchitis is caused by a highly contagious airborne virus. Capable of spreading rapidly where large numbers of dogs are housed—hence the kennel connection, though in all fairness most kennels are extremely vigilant in controlling this problem and ensuring that all residents be vaccinated—the virus causes inflammation of the trachea and larynx, initiating the cough that is its namesake. A runny nose often also accompanies these symptoms.

While not normally a fatal disease, tracheobronchitis can take a heavier toll on puppies and small dogs. It often leaves these animals more susceptible to other infections. Inoculation is the only preventive measure, though it cannot be administered to pregnant females for fear of contaminating unborn pups.

Lyme Disease

This tick-borne disease named for the Connecticut town in which the ailment was first diagnosed in humans, has become increasingly prevalent as a threat to dogs and even more so to their human companions. A vaccine is available for Lyme disease, but because the condition tends to be regional, it is not necessarily a part of a dog's routine vaccine series. Whether or not you live in a known Lyme disease area, you should examine your pet regularly for ticks, especially after spending time outdoors where ticks may reside. Remove any ticks you find promptly (more on this later—see page 84). Should you notice symptoms of Lyme disease in your dog (fever, painful swelling of the joints), prompt veterinary attention is required.

Digestive and Urinary Disorders

Vomiting: Vomiting is not unusual among puppies and young dogs that often eat too much too fast, but violent and frequent vomiting can indeed be a cause for alarm, as it can mean that the animal has ingested poison or some other foreign object, or that an infectious disease has attacked its system. Consult your veterinarian promptly.

Diarrhea: Diarrhea, likewise, is a normal occurrence, but if it becomes a chronic condition for your Doberman, you should have him checked for worms. Contact the veterinarian immediately if your dog has diarrhea tinged with blood or mucus, as this can be a sign of a potentially deadly illness.

Constipation: Logic applies, too, to constipation problems. If the condition persists, reevaluate your dog's diet, which may be too dry for his system. In the worst possible scenario, continuous constipation can also be a signal that the animal has swallowed an indigestible foreign object, in which case surgery may be required.

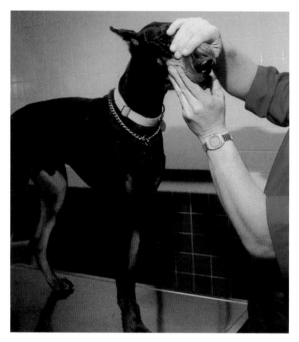

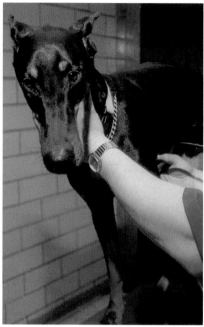

Urination habits: You should also remain attuned to your dog's urination habits, so that you might notice signs of severe and potentially life-threatening urinary tract ailments, such as kidney disease, bladder infections, and bladder stones. Blood in the urine is the most dramatic sign, but look also for a sudden increase in thirst and water intake and a subsequent increase in urination, as well as obvious pain or straining when the dog urinates. All of these are reasons to call the veterinarian. Remember, too, that the sooner you seek treatment, the better chance your dog will survive.

Respiratory Infections

Infections of the larynx and trachea can be related to a variety of different maladies, among them tracheobronchitis, distemper, and pneumonia. Symptoms of the latter condition include high fever, loss of appetite, lethargy, breathlessness, and/or a rattling sound during breathing. Only a veterinarian can make an accurate diagnosis and prescribe the right treatment.

Genetic Conditions

Every breed is plagued by various genetic conditions that seem to run either in certain breeds or in dogs as a whole. Hip dysplasia, for one, is a condition that may appear more frequently in some of the larger breeds (such as the Doberman), but can affect any dog. This is a malformation of the hip joint that can grow more severe and debilitating as a dog ages. The

Once your dog reaches adulthood, he should visit the veterinarian every year for a routine veterinary checkup. This typically consists of, among other procedures, examining the ears, teeth, and mouth, and evaluating the heartbeat and pulse.

Orthopedic Foundation for Animals tests and rates dogs for their hip dysplasia potential. Conscientious breeders supply new puppy buyers with their dogs' OFA status, and they do not breed and show dogs that do not pass the test with flying colors.

Prospective Doberman buyers are also wise to look for puppies whose parents have been evaluated for eye problems by the Canine Eye Registration Foundation. The best breeders will tell you about the need for this, probably before you even ask.

Wobbler syndrome: The same concern applies to wobbler syndrome, a severe spinal abnormality that is, unfortunately, all too common in Doberman Pinschers. Typically diagnosed in Dobermans of about four to six years of age, the affected dog will experience a degeneration in several disks in the neck, resulting in a progressive loss of coordination and a wobbling gait, as well as pain and paralysis. More is yet to be learned about this condition, but theories suggest that though it is probably hereditary, diet may also contribute. Owners are urged not to overnourish a quickly growing young Doberman with rich, energy-packed foods, and certainly not to breed dogs that are either themselves victims of the syndrome or come from affected lines.

Von Willebrand's disease: Von Willebrand's disease, a hereditary blood disorder, is another condition common in Doberman Pinschers. The blood of affected dogs does not clot properly, resulting in nosebleeds, wounds that bleed more than they should, lameness, and severe bruising. Such dogs should not be bred, and ethical breeders know it. Prospective owners need to be aware of this, too, if they are to increase the chances of their choosing a healthy pet.

Dilated cardiomyopathy: Another serious condition that is believed to be hereditary is dilated cardiomyopathy, a fatal heart disease common in Dobermans. Symptoms include shortness of breath, loss of appetite and weight, and coughing, as the heart of the affected dog swells, enlarges, and beats inefficiently. Some dogs exhibit no symptoms at all until the later stages, when heart failure and death are inevitable. When diagnosed early through annual checkups, treatment may help slow the progression, but dogs diagnosed with the disease, or those that come from affected lines, should not be bred.

External Parasites

One area of health care that involves you and the rest of the members of your family as the first line of defense is the prevention of external parasites. External parasites, particularly fleas, ticks, and mites, are more than a nuisance. In some cases, infestation of these pests can lead to health complications that can actually prove fatal to a dog. Even when it doesn't, their presence can make life miserable, both for the dog and his owners, the latter of which can also fall prey to the ensuing plague.

Fleas

Flea shampoos, sprays, and powders are the classic methods of preventing flea infestations in dogs, but in recent years, a revolution has occurred in this area. New products, some of which are applied topically to target adult fleas, some administered orally or by injection to kill flea larvae and eggs, thus preventing them from becoming bloodsucking adults, have changed the playing field considerably in favor of the dog. Some of these products are available over-the-counter, others by prescription from veterinarians.

Yet the basic tenets of overall flea and parasite control remain the same. While you must treat the dog directly to rid the poor animal of fleas, you must address the dog's environment, as well, to prevent reinfestation. Fleas in your Doberman's coat can be disposed of by using one of the new products, and/or specially medicated shampoos, dips, rinses, or even a good old-fashioned flea comb, but there remains the additional problem of dealing with the countless number of eggs the little monsters may leave behind in your pet's bedding and all over your house. These can hatch days, even months, later and start the problem all over again.

For fleas in the home and yard, choose environmental sprays, foggers, and the like that target preadult fleas (eggs and larvae) as well as adults. Read directions carefully, and treat your dog's bedding and all the carpets, furniture, and public areas in your home with an appropriate product. Repeat the treatment as needed. In cases of extreme infestation, you may have to call in a professional exterminator to "debug" your home.

Puppies, pregnant and nursing females, and dogs with compromised immune systems can have problems with flea products, so talk to your veterinarian ahead of time to make sure the products you use on or around your dog and your home are safe as well as effective. These are powerful chemicals you are using, so once you have come up with a game plan for your flea-prevention program, follow the instructions to the letter.

Ticks

Ticks can carry a variety of illnesses, such as Lyme disease, Rocky Mountain spotted fever, and encephalitis (inflammation of the brain). Ticks usually drop onto dogs from bushes and trees with which the animals come into contact and feed on blood—sometimes on the blood of a dog's owners!

Many flea products target both ticks and fleas, but you should also examine your dog carefully from head to toe whenever you visit potentially tick-infested areas. If you discover a tick attached to your dog's skin, first apply oil or one of the specially formulated tick-removal products available at pet supply stores. The tick can then be more easily removed with a pair of tweezers. Never pull on a tick, as its head may snap and remain embedded in the skin, causing pain and inflammation. The correct method is to use a back-and-forth motion.

Mites

Producing a condition known collectively as mange, mites present a slightly different problem. There are so many different kinds of mites—some so small they can only be detected with a microscope—that it is best to let your veterinarian identify them and prescribe proper treatment. Symptoms include shaking and scratching of the ears, an accumulation of dark earwax, intense itching and hair loss, and redness of the skin.

The eradication of mites can be a frustrating endeavor, and you must have a veterinarian's help. Left untreated, mange will spread, so the moment you suspect an infestation, make the call. Once an infestation and the culprit are identified, follow the doctor's orders to the letter. And be patient. Success can take time.

Internal Parasites

Unfortunately, dogs are attractive not only to pests that attack the outside of a dog, but to those that hunger for the warmth within the dog's body, as well. As with the external parasites, you will be best equipped to combat these creatures successfully if you know your enemy.

A curious Doberman can pick up internal parasites just by following its nose around the great outdoors. Have your pet checked regularly, and you can stop an infestation at its earliest stage.

Roundworms et al

The most common internal parasite, roundworms frequently invade a dog's small intestine. White or yellow in color, they can cause

Get to know your dog well—her personality and her habits—and you will recognize quickly even subtle changes in behavior that might indicate illness or injury.

a loss or marked increase of appetite, diarrhea, anal itching, cramps, stomach bloating, a constant lack of energy, and/or paralysis.

Especially dangerous to puppies, roundworm infestation occurs by way of worm eggs that infected dogs pass in their stools, another good reason to keep your Doberman from investigating other dogs' droppings. Several different drugs are available to combat this problem. It is also wise to have your pet's feces examined every six months or so by the veterinarian to make sure the dog is not suffering an infestation of roundworms or any other internal parasites, such as whipworms or hookworms, that make their presence known in the dog's stools.

Tapeworms

This parasite also attacks a dog's small intestine. Transmitted via such intermediary hosts as fleas, lice, rabbits, pigs, and sheep, the worms enter a dog's body in the form of larvae when the animal swallows one of the hosts or eats contaminated meat. Symptoms include weight loss, inflammation of the intestine, muscle cramps, anal itching, and a dull coat. You can also usually see the worms rather easily around the dog's anal area; they resemble white grains of rice. Worming medicines that combat tapeworms are readily available, but the best preventive measure is to avoid giving your dog uncooked meats and to keep the dog as well as his environment parasite-free at all times.

Heartworms

As the name suggests, this notorious parasite attacks the heart and infestation can be fatal. As long as a foot in length (30.5 cm) when fully grown, this parasite is transmitted by mosquitoes that have themselves been infected after biting a dog carrying heartworms.

Symptoms of heartworm infestation are fatigue, nervousness, coughing, breathing difficulties, and a swelling of the legs and feet. Treatment, which must be carried out only in partnership with a veterinarian, can be almost as dangerous as the infestation, as it can result in suffocation if the worms retreat to the lungs and cut off air, or a blockage of blood vessels in the heart after the worms die. Prevention is obviously preferable, and this can be carried out with a prescribed preventive administered once a month. You must first, however, have the dog tested to ensure that he is not already infested before beginning the preventive regimen.

Emergency Care

Dobermans are active, curious dogs that love taking part in family activities. Of course, this can result in accidents and injuries, so you need to be prepared. If your Doberman is injured where no help is available, his survival may depend on your knowledge of first aid.

Remember, however, that though your Doberman may be the love of your life, if he becomes delirious or is suffering great pain, he may instinctively lash out at you while you are attempting to treat him. If someone else is with you, it will be easier to keep the dog under control; otherwise you may have to muzzle the dog temporarily by tying a shirt sleeve or whatever is handy around his snout.

Shock

A state of shock often follows injury or severe fright. A dog that has suffered such trauma and/or blood loss may lapse into shock and lose consciousness. If that occurs, make sure the dog's air passages are clear, and extend the animal's neck to facilitate breathing.

Symptoms of shock include shallow breathing, a weak pulse, pale gums, and dilation of the pupils. Failure of the circulatory system may follow. Immediate action dictates keeping your pet as quiet and as still as possible, and covered, particularly in cold weather, although your ultimate goal must be to get the dog to the hospital immediately.

External Bleeding

If your dog is bleeding from a skin injury, wash the area with soap and water, then apply an antiseptic medication to the wound. If the injury is a large one and looks as though it will need stitches, apply a temporary gauze bandage and immediately seek professional help.

To apply a bandage properly, place a thick layer of sterile gauze over the injured area, winding the bandage tightly enough to stop or at least slow the bleeding. Remove the bandage periodically—every 15 to 20 minutes or so—to prevent excess swelling, and replace it with a new one if the bleeding continues. Never apply cotton to the wound, as it may stick to it.

If a cut is deep and an artery has been severed, the blood will appear bright in color, flowing in time with the dog's heartbeat. Blood from a vein, on the other hand, will be a darker red, and its flow will be steady by comparison. To slow bleeding from an artery, apply pressure between the heart and the wound; where a vein is involved, pressure should be applied below the wound. In either case, get the dog to the veterinarian immediately.

Internal Bleeding

Even if a dog seems to have survived an injury intact, it is still possible that the animal may have sustained internal damage. Signs of internal hemorrhaging include an inability to move or stand up, and a pale gray discoloration of the gums. Bleeding from the nose may signify a head injury. If there is bleeding from the mouth, check both tongue and mouth for cuts. Whenever internal bleeding is suspected, quick veterinary assistance may prove critical to your pet's survival.

Broken Bones

Broken bones are fairly easy to diagnose, even for an amateur. Intense pain and a loss of mobility are the prime indications, and they may be accompanied by signs of shock as well. In the case of a compound fracture, you will be able to see the bone protruding through the skin.

In the event of a break, keep the animal as still as possible, and fashion some kind of stretcher so you can transport the patient to the veterinarian with minimal discomfort. A flat, hard surface makes the best improvised stretcher, but it's unlikely you'll find such an item when you need it most. You may have to make do with a blanket, tent, or other clothlike material. Try to keep the material taut. The dog should be subjected to as little movement as possible.

Canine Bloat

Canine bloat, also known by such official names as gastric dilatation-volvulus or torsion, is a critical condition not uncommon in Dobermans. Though any dog can experience bloat, most large dogs are potential candidates for this deadly condition, which requires immediate emergency medical attention.

Bloat typically occurs when a dog gobbles down his food and then chases his meal with a large ration of water. Gas and/or fluid accumulates in the stomach, which responds by swelling, then rotating, and blocking off any ability for the buildup to dissipate. The blood

From an early age, your Doberman will start looking for potentially health-threatening trouble. Arm yourself with knowledge of canine first aid, and you may just end up one day saving your pet's life.

flow in turn is constricted, and shock can ensue. Without proper treatment, death soon follows. If you notice that your dog appears restless and in pain following a large meal, that he is salivating profusely, and attempting unsuccessfully to defecate or vomit, you need to get him to the veterinarian immediately for treatment, which may require surgery to move the stomach back into position.

✔ To prevent bloat, don't allow your pet to drink large amounts of water or to exercise strenuously immediately before or after eating.

✔ If you own more than one dog, feed the dogs with separate dishes in separate rooms so they don't feel the need to race each other to the bottom of the dish at mealtime.

✔ And finally, divide your dog's daily ration of food into two or three small meals that you offer your pet throughout the day rather than offering one large meal each day.

Burns

Treatment of a burn depends on what caused the burn. Assuming the damage is confined to a small area (larger burn sites require immediate professional attention), burns caused by heat or fire can be treated by applying ice or cold-water compresses, followed by a topical antibiotic. Do not use oil-based preparations.

Burns caused by an acid or chemicals should be flushed with warm water, after which a solution of baking soda may be applied. Call your veterinarian for specific instructions; it will help greatly if you are able to identify the burn-causing agent.

Poisoning

Poisons are another serious threat, for they exist all over the place and in all different

Pesticides and Chemicals

Note that garden-variety pesticides can be poisonous to dogs. If you must use them around the home, do not let your dog come into contact with them for at least two weeks after application. Make sure, too, that all chemicals, such as antifreeze, are stored where the dog cannot get to them, and keep the phone number of the poison control center posted near your telephone. As with so many potential emergency situations, this one, too, can be prevented with a little forethought on the part of the dog owner.

forms. Treatment depends on what type of poison is involved, but in general, symptoms include shivering, panting, retching, vomiting, and, occasionally, convulsions. In extreme cases, coma and death may occur.

If you don't know what kind of poison your dog has ingested, your pet is at a severe disadvantage. With most poisons, it is best to induce vomiting if that is not already occurring. To do this, mix equal parts hydrogen peroxide and water, or two to three tablespoons of salt in a glass of water, and force the dog to drink it. This you can do by raising the animal's head, pulling out his lower lip to form a "gutter" of sorts, and pouring the mixture into it. Unfortunately, though, some poisons, such as gasoline, kerosene, and acids, can do as much damage coming out as they did going in, so forcing your dog to vomit in these cases is *not* recommended.

If you can identify the poison and its original container is within reach, it will likely have antidote instructions on the label. Consider yourself fortunate, but call the veterinarian or the poison control center right away anyhow.

Heatstroke

Heatstroke occurs when a dog is overexposed to the sun, overworked in hot weather, or all too commonly, left too long in a hot car or other confined place that has insufficient air circulation. Without immediate intervention, the condition can be fatal.

A dog suffering from heatstroke will seem faint, and he may have difficulty breathing. Emergency treatment demands that you reduce the animal's body temperature as quickly as possible. Place the dog in a tub or pool filled with cool, not cold, water, or soak him down with a garden hose if one is handy. As this is a bona fide emergency, call the veterinarian as soon as you can.

Heatstroke is, of course, easily prevented. Work your dog outdoors during the cooler hours of the day, make sure he always has access to fresh water and shade, and when the temperature outdoors is even just slightly warm, leave the dog at home when you go out to run your errands.

Choking

Should your dog suddenly start choking and coughing, perhaps pawing at his mouth and shaking his head, he may very well have something lodged in his throat, a potentially life-threatening situation. Open the dog's mouth, pull his tongue out a bit if you can grab hold of it, and see if you can spot the cause of the problem. If you can see a foreign object in the dog's throat, you can try to remove it with your fingers.

Another option for the choking dog is the Heimlich maneuver for dogs. With a dog the size of the Doberman Pinscher, you do this very much as you would with another person. Wrap your arms around the dog just below the rib cage and pull up several times in a row. This should release the offending item from the airway so the dog can resume his breathing. If this doesn't work, your only other option is to get the dog to the veterinarian—immediately!

The Breeding Question

No chapter on Doberman health would be complete without a discussion of breeding. The how-tos of breeding would require an entire volume devoted solely to that subject—and they have many times over. Ethical dog breeders know this, just as they also know that breeding, when done properly, is not a profit-making venture. What moves these people is the desire to improve their breed by striving toward its standard of perfection. Considering the investment in both time and money required to see such an undertaking through, the breeder is lucky to just break even.

Serious breeders view their efforts as a calling, and, frankly, this would not describe most dog owners, even those who love and care for their pets as family members. Far too often, fledgling breeders have no idea what they are getting into: the risks to a mother's health, the precarious futures of the puppies they produce in a world overpopulated by unwanted pure-breds, and the great expenses required to ensure that Mom and puppies remain healthy after whelping. Those ignorant about the nuances of Doberman breeding may not fully understand the long-term genetic ramifications of their actions, the physical and temperament standards involved in choosing breeding stock, the challenge of cropping and docking, and the difficulty of placing such puppies in decent

Everyone loves puppies, but resisting the impulse to breed your dog is one of the kindest steps you can take as an owner. An altered dog lives a more content, healthier, and longer life.

permanent homes. Success for the newcomer requires mentoring from an experienced, ethical breeder, who will typically get involved *only* if he or she believes the breeding pair should be bred in the first place; more often than not, the typical beloved pet should not be.

A major mistake far too many dog owners make is falling for the myths that surround spaying and neutering. These individuals believe a dog will gain weight if he or she is altered (insufficient diet and exercise are what lead to weight gain). They believe that their dog is so wonderful, they are obligated to pro-duce more just like him or her. And they believe the myth that a female should have at least one litter before she is spayed.

What these people need to understand instead is that there are plenty of nice Dober-mans out there in need of good homes—too many, in fact. Most important, they need to understand that their pets, male or female, will not only be better, more contented and devoted companions if they are altered, but they will probably live longer and healthier, as well, as they will not be prone to many types of cancer and other serious conditions that affect intact animals. Free from hormonal impulses, altered animals are more relaxed, more attentive pets. Indeed, spaying and neutering are the most humane and effective preventive steps one can take toward protecting Doberman pets and the well-being of the breed as a whole.

Books

American Kennel Club Staff. *The Complete Dog Book.* New York: Howell Book House, 1998.

Carlson, Delbert G.; James M. Giffin; Liisa Carleson; James Giffin. *Dog Owner's Home Veterinary Handbook* (Third Edition). New York: John Wiley & Sons, 1999.

Coile, Caroline D. *Encyclopedia of Dog Breeds.* Hauppauge, New York: Barron's Educational Series, Inc., 1998.

Fogle, Bruce; Roger Caras; ASPCA Staff. *ASPCA Complete Dog Care Manual.* New York: DK Publishing, 1993.

Monks of New Skete. *How to Be Your Dog's Best Friend* (Second Edition). Lebanon, IN: Little, Brown & Company, 2002.

Palika, Liz. *How to Train Your Doberman Pinscher.* Neptune, New Jersey: TFH Publications, 1999.

Rutherford, Clarice; David H. Neil. *How to Raise a Puppy You Can Live With.* New York: Fine Communications, 2001.

Magazines

American Kennel Club Gazette
www.akc.org
260 Madison Avenue
New York, NY 10016
E-mail: gazette@akc.org

Dogs in Canada
Dogs-in-canada.com
89 Skyway Avenue, Suite 200
Etobicoke, Ontario, Canada M9W 6R4

Dog Fancy
Dogs USA
Dog World
www.animalsnetwork.com
Fancy Publications
3 Burroughs
Irvine, CA 92618

Organizations
The American Kennel Club
www.akc.org
260 Madison Avenue
New York, NY 10016

All the forms and information you need to register your Doberman with the AKC are available at **www.akc.org.**

The ideal lifestyle for a Doberman includes time spent both indoors with the family and outdoors in a safely confined space.

Canadian Kennel Club
www.ckc.ca/default-refresh.asp
89 Skyway Avenue, Suite 100
Etobicoke, Ontario, Canada M9W 6R4

Canine Eye Registration Foundation
http://vet.purdue.edu/~yshen/cerf.html
c/o Lynn Hall
Purdue University
625 Harrison Street
W. Lafayette, IN 47907-2026

The Doberman Pinscher Club of America
www.dpca.org
36277 80th Street East
Little Rock, CA 93543-2519

The Doberman Pinscher Foundation of America
www.dpfa.org

The Kennel Club (Great Britain)
www.the-kennel-club.org.uk
1 Clarges Street
London, England W1J 8AB

Orthopedic Foundation for Animals
www.offa.org
2300 E. Nifong Boulevard
Columbia, MO 65201-3856

Photo Credits

Pets by Paulette: 5, 10, 22, 23, 34, 35, 36, 40, 47, 49, 50, 55, 57, 58, 63, 65, 67, 78, 79; Kent Dannen: 2, 6, 9, 11, 15, 16, 19, 24, 28, 31, 42, 43, 62, 68, 77, 85, 86, 91, 93; Tara Darling: 8, 17, 20, 21 (top), 25, 26, 29, 30, 38, 51, 56, 61, 64, 71, 73, 74, 80, 88, 92; Norvia Behling: 4, 14, 21 (bottom), 44, 45, 59; Paulette Johnson: 33, 39, 54; Susan Green: 46, 48; Eugene Butenas & Larry Naples (LCA Photography): 82, 83.

Cover Photos

Front cover, back cover, and inside back cover: Pets by Paulette. Inside front cover: Kent Dannen.

Important Note

This book is concerned with the selection, keeping, and raising of Doberman Pinschers. The authors and publisher think it is important to point out that the advice and information for Doberman Pinscher maintenance applies to healthy, normally developed dogs. Anyone who acquires an adult dog or one from an animal shelter must consider that the animal may have behavioral problems and may, for example, bite without provocation. Such anxiety biters are dangerous for the owners as well as the general public.

We also advise using caution in the association of children with dogs, in meetings with other dogs, and in exercising the dog without a leash.

About the Authors

Betsy Sikora Siino is the award-winning author/ editor of more than 20 books and hundreds of articles on dogs, horses, wild predators, and pets of every shape and size.

Raymond Gudas, former editor of *Pet Age* magazine, has written extensively on animal topics. He is the author of Barron's *Gerbils: A Complete Pet Owner's Manual.*

All inquiries should be addressed to:
Barron's Educational Series, Inc.
250 Wireless Boulevard
Hauppauge, NY 11788
www.barronseduc.com

ISBN-13: 978-0-7641-2857-8
ISBN-10: 0-7641-2857-4

Library of Congress Catalog Card No. 2004059969

Library of Congress Cataloging-in-Publication Data
Siino, Betsy Sikora.
    Doberman pinschers / Betsy Sikora-Siino, Raymond Gudas.
        p. cm.
    Rev. ed. of: Doberman pinschers / Raymond Gudas. 2nd ed. c1995.
    Includes index.
    ISBN 0-7641-2857-4
    1. Doberman pinscher. I. Gudas, Raymond. II. Gudas, Raymond. Doberman pinschers. III. Title.

SF429.D6S56 2005
636.73'6—dc22   2004059969

Printed in China
9 8 7 6